THE SACRED WORK OF GRANDPARENTS RAISING GRANDCHILDREN

Elaine K. Williams

BALBOA.
PRESS

A DIVISION OF HAY HOUSE

Balboa Press books may be ordered through booksellers or by contacting:

Balboa Press
A Division of Hay House
1663 Liberty Drive
Bloomington, IN 47403
www.balboapress.com
1-(877) 407-4847

Because of the dynamic nature of the Internet, any web addresses or links contained in this book may have changed since publication and may no longer be valid. The views expressed in this work are solely those of the author and do not necessarily reflect the views of the publisher, and the publisher hereby disclaims any responsibility for them.

The author of this book does not dispense medical advice or prescribe the use of any technique as a form of treatment for physical, emotional, or medical problems without the advice of a physician, either directly or indirectly. The intent of the author is only to offer information of a general nature to help you in your quest for emotional and spiritual well-being. In the event you use any of the information in this book for yourself, which is your constitutional right, the author and the publisher assume no responsibility for your actions.

Any people depicted in stock imagery provided by Thinkstock are models, and such images are being used for illustrative purposes only.
Certain stock imagery © Thinkstock.

Book Cover and photographs by Allyson Williams-Yee

ISBN: 978-1-4525-3677-4 (e)
ISBN: 978-1-4525-3675-0 (sc)
ISBN: 978-1-4525-3676-7 (hc)

Library of Congress Control Number: 2011913056

Printed in the United States of America

Balboa Press rev. date: 8/05/2011

READER REVIEWS

"Elaine's ground breaking examination of parenting grandparents combines her extensive professional expertise and her passion for the well being of children. Elaine articulates the impact of grandparents thrust into the role of parenting their grandchildren and gives them hope. The truth telling of the stories captures the essence of this staggering, social phenomenon."
Rebecca P. Fitton, M.A., M.B.A., Santa Fe, New Mexico

"Someone needed to do a thoughtful, intelligently written and caring book on a sensitive, even difficult subject, grandparents raising grandchildren, and now we have it. Elaine K. Williams was the perfect person to do just that. She adds common sense with a common touch. What a gift she has given us all. Perhaps, we may better comprehend what is happening, why it is happening and how to face this growing social phenomena. Elaine makes you feel elevated, reflective and inspires you to ask "what you can do."
Dr. Richard Steckel, Educator, Denver, Colorado

"This book is essential reading for grandparents from Navajo country. Grandparents have helped raise their grandchildren for centuries but the modern world presents new challenges and we look for ideas and support from others in this sacred duty. Thank you."
Gloria J. Emerson, M.Ed., Educator, Poet, and Painter, Shiprock, New Mexico

Elaine K. Williams presents powerful and insightful descriptions of the work facing grandparents who have taken on the role of parenting. Given the statistics, perhaps we in education, should reconfigure our courses relating to families and schools to include grandparents. This book, through the power of storytelling, provides educators invaluable information about the emotional needs, challenges and solutions for both the children and grandparents who are now living together.
Judith Gold, M.A., Bank Street College of Education, New York, New York

In the complex world in which we live, Elaine K. William's book offers the knowledge, understanding and important tools for grandparents and their grandchildren to navigate the often difficult waters when roles unexpectedly shift. Such changes often put kids and adults in unknown territory. Elaine's great wisdom comes to the rescue with insightful, concrete information to survive with dignity and raise happy, healthy children.
Louise Hublitz, M.A., School Counselor, Flagstaff, Arizona

"Ideas, alternatives, new ways of seeing things, new ways of acting in the world—all these things require creative thinking. Elaine has done the thinking and captured it in this book. She offers fresh new ways of thinking and fresh alternatives to help grandparents successfully raise their grandchildren. These simple, yet powerful approaches are relevant to anyone directly or indirectly involved with being a kinship caregiver."
Jean Carroccio, M.S.W., M.P.A. Edward de Bono Certified: Creative and Perceptual Thinking Systems, Denver, Colorado

Dedicated to
My sister, Cynthia....with love

ACKNOWLEDGMENTS

Without my community of family and friends and a sense of Spirit in my life, this book would not have been written.

My heartfelt gratitude to my family---to my daughters, Laura and Kimberly, for their constant encouragement and astute suggestions and edits on my many drafts; to my daughter Allyson for her photography and artistic and personal support; to my granddaughters, Shelby, Elizabeth, and Megan for helping me understand the magic world of technology and the uniqueness of your generation; and to my youngest grandchildren, Andrew and Sophie, who supported me with hugs and smiles when I was tired and crabby!

Deep appreciation to my sister Cynthia, and her family---her daughter, Amy, her son Michael and his wife Cindy, who helped edit my final draft; her grandchildren, Jordan and McKenzee. Thank you all for your open hearts.

Dr. Caron Goode, I could not have finished this book without you, your support, your being my teacher. Without you, I would not have believed I could write a book but you pulled me out of that pit more times than I can count---and so gently. "Aho!"

To my Spirit Sister, Rebecca P. Fitton, I thank you for your "cave" and am indebted to the unwavering support you offered throughout the five years it took me to complete my interviews and write this book. Your unique spirit, insistence and guidance were a boost to my spirit.

Many thanks also to four shining stars of encouragement, Dee Dee Raap, Jean Carroccio, Kapila Wewegama, and Frank Williams.

May life's finest blessings flow to each of you and to those I have not named who provided constant support.

FOREWORD

We are missing a generation of parents, and grandparents have stepped into the roles of parenting, Estimates reveal that 7 million grandparents have stretched beyond the generation gap to embrace and care for their children's children. They do this on fixed incomes and with little community or government support.

Here's the good news. I've never met a more savvy, educated group of men and women who are fighting for their grandchildren and forming grass roots support networks. My friend and colleague, Elaine K. Williams watched this phenomenon grow and in her travels interviewed sixty plus grandparents and a handful of non-profit associations, like AARP, Generations United, and Child Welfare League of America, who spearheaded these support networks.

The grandparent/grandchild relationship is indeed special. I had a very close relationship with my Grandpa. I was Grandpa's girl. I rode his work horse, played in his barn, and loved to hang out with him. Every time I asked if I could stay overnight, he agreed; yet I never spent the entire night because I always woke up homesick. At 2 am, Grandpa would take me home!

Every child needs a grandparent like mine. The grandparenting relationship brings unconditional love, a feeling of connection and safety, fun and trust that makes being a child a magical adventure.

Now, when the magic disappears, grandkids need their grandparents to parent them in a world where it hasn't always been safe---where people don't always do what they said they would do.

What relationship offers the opportunity to share a legacy and create memories while building skills and setting boundaries that help our children achieve the success in life they deserve? What relationship is more sacred to a little girl who counted on her grandfather to always be there for her?

Elaine K. Williams, in her new book, *The Sacred Work of Grandparents Raising Grandchildren*, offers the amazing combination of how to love grandchildren while being their parent. It is a sacred journey, indeed.

As a member of the generation of grandparents who are now raising their children, Elaine understands in a deeply meaningful way how vital parenting grandparents are to their grandchildren. Her genuine interest in every family member's story took her through 11 states while sharing many a cup of tea around kitchen tables. Elaine's natural curiosity and empathy through her extensive interviews of grandparents raising their grandchildren opened doorways of awareness about their sadness, scars, sacrifices and solutions that we need to know, discuss, and bring into the open.

Through Elaine's book, we now have a solid foundation to understand how we in the helping professions can assist families through these transitions. Elaine provides suggestions and answers that help both grandchildren and grandparents understand the dynamics behind their many challenges. Resources that address psycho-emotional needs as well as the economic and social needs of family members are practical and accessible.

As grandparents we empower our grandchildren by teaching values through words, actions and family traditions to help them grow, achieve, explore and return to the roots of their family These priceless values provide the bridge to connect generations and are the foundation for strong families.

Grandparents' work is sacred indeed. Elaine's message will guide, renew, refresh and restore grandparents raising their grandchildren because her words are grounded in research and fueled by a love that makes a very real difference in the world for those of us blessed with her friendship. My friend's purpose in life is to help you, the grandparent, take the sacred journey of parenting your grandchildren.

Dee Dee Raap, author
Dear Mom: Remembering, Celebrating, Healing
Find Your Pink Flamingos: Celebrating the Gifts of a Mom

CONTENTS

INTRODUCTION

I dedicate this book to every parenting grandparent, whose work is both sacred and noble.

I have written this book to affirm these grandparents' many sacrifices on behalf of their grandchildren, as well as to highlight the growing number of grandparents involved in raising their grandchildren full- or part-time. In addition, I intended for this book to inform and inspire parenting grandparents, and also to offer them a way to connect with one another.

The book identifies the many challenges faced by parenting grandparents, their adult children, grandchildren, and, in some instances, great-grandchildren. It also offers solutions, suggestions, and resources to help parenting grandparents understand the dynamics behind their stories, as well as the stresses and challenges.

Implicit in understanding what it means for grandparents to raise their grandchildren is an appreciation for the cost that this growing trend has on our society, our elders, and, most important, our children. According to the U.S. Census Bureau, 9 percent of all children living in the United States lived with a grandparent in the year 2009.[1] "In all, roughly 7 million U.S. children live in households that include at least one grandparent, according to a Pew Research Center analysis from 2008. Of that number, 2.9 million were being raised primarily by their grandparents — up 16 percent from 2000, with a 6 percent surge just from 2007 to 2008."[2]

The reasons why so many children are being raised by their grandparents are complex. In 1998, nearly 44 percent of youngsters were living with their grandparents because of the children's parents' substance abuse. Out of that number, 28 percent were victims of child abuse, neglect, or improper attention. Another 11 percent lived with their grandparents because of the death of one or both of the parents.[3]

This book will explore these and other reasons behind the significant rise in the number of grandparents raising their grandchildren. The importance of this book lies in the major impact that this trend has on the American family, suggesting the fragility of this foundational unit of our society.

This book utilizes the power of storytelling to illustrate the fortitude, commitment, and sacrifices that parenting grandparents demonstrate on behalf of their grandchildren. These grandparents' stories that I have included represent the stories of *all* parenting grandparents, and they are stories that inspire and command the respect of all who read them.

> *Ann, a sixty-four-year-old widow, works full-time and is a mother and grandmother. Her son and a daughter, Sam and Susan, are forty-year-old twins. Sam is married, and he and his wife work full-time in their chosen careers. Susan and her children—fourteen-year-old James and four-year-old Kayli—intermittently live with Ann.*

> *Ann is one of several million grandparents raising or helping to raise their grandchildren. Her husband died three years ago, but she has had very little time to grieve for her loss. Susan had numerous medical problems following the birth of Kayli, and these problems continue to this day. Both Susan and James are pre-diabetic, and this presents additional challenges.*

When Ann comes home from work, she is never sure what awaits her. James, who lives with Ann full-time during the school year, will need help with his homework. Depending on how Susan feels that day, both she and Kayli may also be at Ann's home and need her help.

The "busyness" of caring for everyone, budgeting to provide for all their needs (which includes paying for medical bills not covered by insurance), and worrying about their health and well-being, are just a few of the stressors Ann faces daily.

Ann's situation is not an atypical one for grandparents raising their grandchildren; sadly, it is quite typical. (In part II of chapter 4, we will take a more detailed look at the story of Ann and her family.)

The incidence of grandparents parenting their grandchildren on a full- or part-time basis has reached epidemic proportions in the United States. Of the 2.9 million grandparents reporting they are responsible for their grandchildren living with them; 29% of these grandparents are African American; 17% are Hispanic/Latino; 2% are American Indian or Alaskan Native; 3% are Asian; and 47% are White.[4]

The youngsters of today live in a world that is drastically different from the one in which their grandparents were raised. Bridging the gap created by these differences takes energy, education, insight, understanding, and adaptability. The first objective of this book is to help build the understanding that is necessary in order for such disparate generations to coexist in the same household.

This book's second objective is to examine the developmental growth stages of both children and adults. This examination will assist grandparents in understanding the chronological, psychological, emotional, and social stages children pass through as they grow. Also, it will help grandparents set age-appropriate expectations for their grandchildren, so that these youngsters can be successful in meeting the challenges of each developmental life stage.

The third objective of this book is to help grandparents understand the dynamics behind the emotional and behavioral challenges that many of their grandchildren exhibit. This book will explore the deep impact that trauma has on children and teens, and it will offer suggestions to help grandparents cope with these challenges.

Another objective is to explore the complex issue of the deep physical and emotional losses and associated grief that both grandparents and grandchildren face. When grandparents become parents to their grandchildren, this forces them to give up their grandparenting role—and all the pleasure and privileges that come with that role. This creates a loss for both the grandparent and the grandchild, and it is important to grieve for that loss.

Furthermore, grandparents must deal with the son or daughter who is the grandchildren's absent parent, as well as the situations, issues, losses, and challenges that prevented him or her from raising the children. These challenges are usually extremely difficult problems or misfortunes that have affected the lives of everyone in the family, either directly or indirectly. These problems or misfortunes may include lethal or debilitating injuries, crime, addictions, chronic or terminal illness, mental illness, unemployment, promiscuity, divorce, death, abuse/ neglect, or home foreclosures.

Grandparents often experience the judgment of others in regard to their role of being a parenting grandparent. Frequent criticisms include, "being too old to raise a child" or "having been a failure as a parent" with their own, now adult-child, who struggles with their own life circumstances." In addition, grandparents may have to give up their retirement dreams and/or relationships with their friends who still want to travel and socialize, while the parenting grandparents cannot. While parenting grandparents have proved to be quite resilient and resourceful, all these stressors have a profound impact on their lives.

The grandchildren also have many difficulties to deal with when their grandparents become their parents. Many of these children have been abused, neglected, abandoned, or rejected by their biological parents. Others may feel abandoned because their parent(s) died of a sudden or chronic illness, or as the result of an accident, disaster, etc. As previously mentioned, these children have also lost the relationship with their grandparents as grandparents—a loss that troubles both generations.

Most grandparents either already live on fixed incomes or expect to soon retire and live on fixed incomes. Many of us have recently experienced considerable financial losses to retirement savings, pensions, 401(k) plans, and more. Significantly, the economic crisis, and its impact on our financial institutions, has lingered sufficiently to further intensify the challenge of managing the financial costs of raising children—again.

The one constant of raising children of any generation is the money it costs to educate, clothe, feed, and care for them. Additional costs that frustrate a budget include dental and medical expenses, health-insurance premiums, and prescription costs (for both the children and the grandparents raising them). In addition, the ever-rising costs of food, fuel, electricity, etc., make an already challenging situation even more difficult. To put all this another way, it is hard enough for working parents raising children today, let alone retired or about-to-retire grandparents.

Thus, the final objective of this book is to look at the complex issue of helping parenting grandparents find and access available community resources. More state resources are available now than ever before, but these remain inadequate. Also, many states offer support groups for parenting grandparents. Some of these groups are strong and very proactive, and they have been successful in advocating for the passage of both state and federal legislation to support grandparents raising their grandchildren.

To make this book as useful and effective as possible, each chapter begins by stating its purpose. Again, the stories included illustrate insights that are real and relevant for readers. After some in-depth analysis, the book offers solutions for grandparents, as well as for the grandchildren when appropriate and applicable. Each chapter (and, in some cases, each part within a chapter) ends with a section called "Gentle Reminders," which highlights the significant ideas discussed in that chapter.

Furthermore, regarding the grandparents' stories, every story included in this book is real (with names and places changed). The sixty-plus grandparents interviewed represent diverse racial and ethnic groups from across the United States in order to resonate more fully with all readers, and also to clarify the themes, lessons, and information discussed in the book.

The grandparents interviewed range in age from thirty-nine to eighty-five. Again, all the names have been changed, even though most grandparents gave permission to use their real names. Every grandparent interviewed did so with the hope of helping other grandparents in similar situations.

The grandchildren interviewed also were willing to share their experiences and pain. Their stories show anxiety, fear, and frustration, as well as courage and determination.

A small number of adult children interviewed also chose to share their stories. These are parents who chose or were forced to give guardianship of their children to their own parents so their children could be raised in a safe, secure home. These adult children frequently face judgment; society and other people label them as lazy, deviant, irresponsible, uncaring, and so on. Interviewing them allowed for a deeper understanding of their internal chaos. Reading their stories broadens our perspective and heightens our understanding, not just of their difficult journeys, but of their children's and parents' difficult journeys, as well (that is, the grandchildren's and grandparents').

Finally, some state and federal legislators, as well as board members and employees of many national and state organizations, agreed to share information about this growing social trend. In particular, Generations United, AARP, and the Children's Defense Fund were very helpful in providing national data and the most recent research on parenting grandparents, whom these organizations also refer to as "kinship caregivers".

I wish to acknowledge everyone who assisted me so that I could provide a solid foundation of research and information for this book; I am grateful to all of you.

I also want to personally thank each grandparent who shared his or her story, pain, and vulnerability. The deep love between these grandparents and their grandchildren is evident. Their stories—but, even more so, their commitment to their grandchildren—have brought profound meaning to this book.

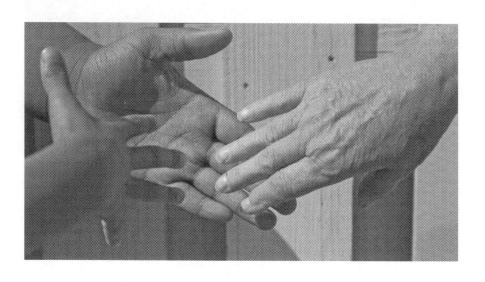

1
THE GENERATIONAL DIVIDE

PART I: YOU SAY BOOTS, AND I SAY GALOSHES

The first part of this chapter will take a lighthearted look at a few of the generational issues that might challenge or support you and your grandchildren as you raise them.

To begin with, it is essential to understand the influence that the Technological/Information Age has on our grandchildren. While every generation has some similarities with and differences from the one that preceded it, the surge of information that has resulted from rapid technological advances has influenced our grandchildren's generation in an unprecedented way. These advances continue to swiftly and inevitably change our world. We need to remember that we knew a different world; our grandchildren did not.

Our grandchildren's access to knowledge and information is phenomenal, and the means to that information—the computer and Internet—can be very isolating for them and very daunting for us. One of the major characteristics of our grandchildren's generation is that they learn and work alone on their computers. They will often text instead of talk on the phone. This is a generation learning to work alone, enjoying autonomy, unencumbered by group or social give-and-take. This can be liberating yet isolating at the same time.

The "computerese" that our grandchildren speak is like a foreign language to grandparents. In addition, an assortment of expensive and complicated high-tech gadgets has flooded the market, and our grandkids often feel they must own these items—all of them! These devices range from MP3 players to mini-DVD players, to all types of gaming systems, to cell phones and smartphones with built-in cameras and Internet access, to scanners, digital cameras, e-readers, tablet computers, and more. (By the time this book goes to press, the high-tech product line will have expanded even further.)

Suffice it to say that, when we were our grandchildren's age, none of these items existed. In fact, in the 1940s, we did not even have television. In the '50s, a few families had a black-and-white television with a screen about ten inches wide. Today, we see plasma and flat-screen televisions as big as fifty-two inches, with built-in DVRs that can record programs even when the television is off. Some grandparents struggled to learn how to master the VCR, the technology of which would be equivalent to that of a "relic" or "fossil" to their grandchildren. Most Americans had three main channels (networks) to watch during the '50s, '60s, and even into the'70s. The'80s, '90s, and turn of the millennium brought cable television, and later, satellite. Now hundreds of channels are at our fingertips, depending on which cable or satellite service you purchase. In addition, today's TV sets are connected to DVD units, sound systems, and more.

Television is just one example of the vast differences between grandparents' and grandchildren's generations. Let's step back in time and look at the values that guided us as we grew up and those that guide our grandchildren today. Let's also compare the environment that influenced each generation—ours and theirs.

This new environment can be daunting to our generation. It is very fast paced compared to our own slower paced environment, and so, it feels very different. Having to leave our comfort zone can be a challenge for both adult and child. But we need to look at how we can build a values bridge, so that grandparents and grandchildren can find some common ground of understanding and mutuality. Most humans assign a high worth to values, because our values are the foundation for how we live; they influence our choices and help us decide what is moral or immoral. Our values determine what we stand for and what we believe in. This chapter will attempt to answer the question: Is there a difference between the values that we elders grew up with and those with which today's children are growing up?

If we took our grandchildren to the Smithsonian Institute in Washington, DC, they would see replicas and relics of the world in which we grew up. Some of our grandchildren would be able to identify some of these relics, but others would not. If we fast-forwarded time, and our grandchildren took us to the Smithsonian to see the world in which they are growing up, many elders would be unable to identify what they were looking at—and, even more important, many would be unable to identify what that specific object does.

The rate of change and advancement is stunning, and, as grandparents raising our grandchildren, we need to bridge the gaps in our knowledge of today's world.

For instance, do you know what an iPhone looks like, or could you work a PlayStation? Most of us could definitely identify a computer, but do you know what Facebook, Twitter, or YouTube is? Could you use an iPod or send or respond to a text? How can we grandparents effectively communicate with our grandchildren when our words, terminology, and methods are so different?

> The important thing to remember is that neither world— ours nor theirs—is better or worse, right or wrong. They are the worlds that have evolved as science, industry, education, math, creativity, and human beings have evolved. It's important not to judge either world, and also not to be afraid of the new world that we are already in or the future that we move toward daily. Instead, we need to acknowledge technology for its strengths and recognize that the foundation of today's world was built on the discoveries and creative solutions shaped and formed during our youth. Life evolves, and we must evolve with it.

I am not sure that it is a correct assumption to say our world was simpler than our grandchildren's is. This is because, as previously indicated, this world is all they know. However, it would be correct to say that our world was simpler for us than their world is for us; and our world was as complicated for our own grandparents as our grandchildren's world is for us. All this illustrates that one of the bridges needed here is an understanding of each other's worlds. We also need to acknowledge that what is familiar to us as human beings is also what is comfortable for us. Change is hard because it requires us to learn and adapt in order to grow.

My older granddaughters—ages eighteen, sixteen, and thirteen—all love to hear stories of my childhood. They are incredulous when I tell them that it was a very big deal when my dad walked into the house with a ten-inch, black-and-white television in 1951. They laugh when they go into my garage and see my old Royal typewriter—and when I tell them that I was able type fifty-five words a minute using it. They are astonished when I tell them that, for some people, being able to type fast was the difference between getting and not getting a job. They also laugh when I tell them that, before we got our TV, we would sit by the radio as a family on Sunday afternoons listening to "The Shadow," which was a peak moment during my family's weekend. Other high points included going on picnics, swimming at a lake, taking long drives to nowhere in particular, visiting with extended family, and playing stickball or Kick the Can in the alley using garbage cans as bases.

My granddaughters—and my daughters, too, for that matter—all smile when I ask for a "ballpoint" instead of a pen, or when I refer to a notebook as a "tablet," blush as "rouge," pants as "slacks," or a hoodie as a "sweatshirt." They snicker when I ask them if they want to go to the show instead of to the "movies," or when I call their capri pants "pedal pushers." They really chuckle if I refer to boots as "galoshes," although I must admit that *galoshes* is a funny word. I might add that the fact that we wore these galoshes over our shoes is unimaginable to them.

They also giggle out loud at the image of an elderly woman with white hair, some thirty or forty years ago, who rinsed her hair with bluing to "brighten" the white, which often tinged it pale blue or lavender. Today, that same woman would simply color her hair whatever shade she chose, never admitting that it was really gray, silver, or white. These differences might seem small, even insignificant, but they represent different eras—a different way of greeting the world, seeing the world, and being in the world.

Another very different thing about today's world is that young folks—both our grandchildren *and* our adult children—love to abbreviate words and use acronyms. They don't write out "laugh out loud," just LOL! They don't write "by the way," just BTW. My oldest daughter recently sent me an e-mail using BTW. When I e-mailed her back, I asked, "By the way, what does BTW mean?" We both had a good laugh over that one!

My grandson, who is seven years old, would not know what I was talking about if I mentioned encyclopedias, 45 rpm records, VHS, or LPs—let alone galoshes! Even if I were to mention these items when he is older, they will be unfamiliar to him. About the only thing I feel we will have in common is the number-two pencil. This old-fashioned device is still around and still used for computerized tests, such as SATs or ACTs.

> It is important that we share with our grandchildren the world we grew up in. Doing so tells them something about who we are; consequently, doing so gives our grandchildren knowledge about who they are. It tells them something about the family they belong to, and also about what influenced us and made us who we are today.
>
> I suggest that grandparents and their grandchildren make time every week or so to tell one another real stories about their lives, from both the present and the past. Take time to imagine the future together. Take time to help

grandchildren understand that, despite the ways in which the world changes, relationships with family, friends, and people will still be the most important part of their lives. These sharing sessions don't have to take a lot of time, which is a precious commodity—you will actually be amazed at how much you can share with each other in fifteen minutes. Remember to also take time to ask your grandchildren to tell you about their world. In doing so, you'll learn a lot and also enable your grandkids to feel like they are teaching you something.

Most important of all, the grandchildren will realize that their grandparents are interested in knowing how the world is affecting them, the future generation. These kinds of exchanges can be a lot of fun, and they are the start of the bridge that we must build between the two generations.

One of the gifts we elders have received is the wisdom that allows us to know what is important in life. Even when cars will drive and park themselves, computers will perform all work in a virtual setting, airplanes will fly around the world in a few hours, and spaceships will take people on vacations to locales in outer space, nothing will take the place of human interaction. The most important part of our world will still and always be about building and nurturing our relationships.

The human heart needs connection and love. The human spirit requires a sense of belonging and inspiration. Technology will never replace or meet those intrinsic human needs; thus, as grandparents, the essential things that we can offer our grandchildren are wisdom and all the love in our hearts. Wisdom provides a wonderful balance and contrast to technology, and this is the bridge that can connect our generational worlds, which seem to be thirty to fifty years apart.

If we worry that, as grandparents, we cannot traverse our grandchildren's world, we should remember that we have the one precious resource we need: our grandchildren, who love leading us through the intricate world of odd words and exotic objects that do marvelous things—and they will do so with pride.

My sixteen-year-old granddaughter taught me how to text on my iPhone, and my thirteen-year-old granddaughter taught me how to create a PowerPoint presentation on the computer. These two new skills have made my life so much easier and it created an even deeper bond between us. Even better, they both taught me how to use Skype. Now I Skype with my granddaughter away at college, their oldest sister, and get to see her by using the video camera on my computer, let alone talk with her. It's like magic!

The world of the computer, the Internet, social media, texting, and instant messaging is a fast-moving, fast-changing one. Accepting and adapting to this frenetic world of our grandkids is important, both for them and for us, because: (1) it inserts us into our grandchildren's world; (2) they can be our teachers, which gives us another type of connection with them; (3) it is far easier to influence our grandkids when we allow them to influence us; (4) they get to see and experience the meaningful effort we are making to understand the world in which they are growing up; (5) we might want to buy them a computer or a tech toy, and how can we do that if we don't know they exist?; and, (6) we want to ensure their safety and well-being in life and online, and we cannot do that if we don't understand or embrace technology.

Although I have treated technology with light humor for the most part, it is important for us to know what our grandchildren need in order for them to keep up with the world around them. For instance, computers are no longer an optional purchase for children. Our grandchildren need to own or have regular access to computers because so much of what they need to learn is computerized. A child or teen who does not own or have access to a computer is at a serious disadvantage in school and in life. Also, many teachers stay in touch with parents via e-mail, and parenting grandparents need to be able to access updates on their students' progress in this way, as opposed to meeting with the teacher in person.

Computer prices have come down significantly since their introduction. Secondhand computers are usually inexpensive and often sufficient for our grandchildren's needs. Businesses change their computers frequently in order to keep up with technology, and many are willing to donate their computers. If you belong to a grandparent support group, encourage the group to contact local businesses to see what might be available.

This chapter affirms the many ways we can bridge the world we grew up in and our grandchildren's world. In later chapters, as we look at life transitions, we will further expand on all this. For now, here are some things to remember.

Gentle Reminders

1. Appreciating some of the similarities and differences between our own world and that of our grandchildren is an important way to build a bridge of understanding between our generations—and between our grandchildren and ourselves.

2. Grandchildren love the stories of their grandparents' own youth and childhood, so make storytelling an important part of your time together. Sharing your story will also give them a sense of belonging to a unique and special heritage.

3. The human heart always needs love and a sense of belonging and connection. Love is the most important gift you can bestow upon your grandchildren.

4. Wherever technology takes our world, building and nurturing human relationships will always remain vital parts of living in a meaningful way.

PART II: VALUES AND BELIEFS THAT BRIDGE GENERATIONS

Earlier, I referred to the need to bridge generations through mutual values. One value that crosses generations is the importance of family. Grandchildren who come from fractured families need to experience healthy, functional family relationships. Their natural need to feel that they have roots, that they belong to a family, must be satisfied in a loving, safe, and accepting environment. As you raise your grandchildren, satisfying this need is your gift to them.

The family of today is not the same family in which grandparents grew up. In the old days, family members lived in close proximity, often in the same household. I lived in a four-flat home (also referred to as a "four-family house"). My parents, my sister and I lived in one flat; my grandparents, in another flat; an aunt and uncle in another; and close friends in the last. Other close relatives lived just three blocks away, and several cousins lived within a mile of our house.

Now families are spread all over the country and the world. Children's contact with extended family often occurs only by phone and over the Internet; social media and online telecommunications give many children greater access to extended family than they had ten years ago. Some children only see their grandparents once a year and may know very little about their aunts and uncles.

My maternal grandparents were, and remain, my heroes. They were the most important influence in my life. Even as a teen, I admired them. They were immigrants from Poland, and I can remember how much I respected their courage for coming to this country when they were fifteen years old, knowing they might never see their families again. Their bravery has influenced my life in many ways. I often compare the risks that I must consider taking with the risk that they took when they came to America—no matter what risk I deliberate, it pales in comparison to theirs.

All grandparents continually impart their values and beliefs to their grandchildren, whether we do so consciously or unconsciously. Even more so, as parenting grandparents, you give your grandchildren a family circle, wherein they are very important members; they belong in, and to, this circle. Your commitment to them creates a commitment to being a family, where, together, you live by and share your core values and beliefs.

In 2004, I attended the national gathering celebrating grandparents who are raising their grandchildren. It took place in front of the Capitol in Washington, DC. Senator Hillary Clinton (D-New York, at the time; now Secretary of State) spoke at the gathering, and so did an eighteen-year-old grandchild whose grandparents sat in the audience.

I don't recall everything Senator Clinton had to say, but my heart still recalls that granddaughter's words about the grandparents who raised her. She had just received a scholarship to start college, and she profusely thanked her grandparents for their love, their patience, and their sacrifices. Speaking plainly and simply, she said, "Grandma and Granddaddy, without you, I would not be standing here today. Without you, I would not know who I am. I plan to make you proud of me, because that is the only way I can thank you for what you have given me."

Not a dry eye remained in the audience after she spoke.

When raising children, the heart must be present. Grandparents' finest gift to their grandkids is to create an environment where these youngsters feel safe to express their hearts to the world, because this leads to a sense of unity with others, as well as a sense of internal and external well-being. This well-being is often called "paying it forward," because, when grown, these children will give back to life the love that they received from you.

Although we may be able to define values in similar ways, we generally express them in many different ways, especially in terms of our behavior. These behavioral differences, vis-à-vis our values, are rooted in culture, ethnicity, beliefs, and environment, all of which influence the different generations.

Let's consider work values. Nearly 50 million Americans were born to the Silent Generation in America, from the beginning of 1925 until about 1944. About 95 percent of the people of that generation are retired at this point. In a few short years, virtually no one from the Silent Generation will command an industry, a battlefield, or anything at all. This generation that Tom Brokaw wrote about in his book, *The Greatest Generation,* believed in receiving pay for a "hard day's work." This meant showing up on time, leaving on time, working without distractions or extended lunch hours, knowing what you are doing, and doing what you know. This worldview also meant retiring at a certain age and finally beginning to enjoy life. This generation lived through the deprivation of the Great Depression and World War II, and so a structured, predictable, rule-oriented approach to life suited their needs. Role responsibilities for being a husband or wife, or a father or mother, were simple and clear. A set of defined boundaries and expectations reflected this generation's values and beliefs, and it also determined how members of this generation actualized their values and beliefs.[5]

The Silent Generation gave birth to the generation known as the Baby Boomers. Born between 1946 and 1964, Boomers view work as a social-networking opportunity. They require work to be meaningful, and they have a high need to learn new information while they are working. Boomers look at retirement very differently from the way that their parents did. For them relaxing is about volunteering, continuous learning, and spending their time in meaningful ways.

One of the unique features of Boomers is that they tend to think of themselves as part of a special generation that is very different from those that came before. By the sheer force of their numbers, the Boomers were, and are, a demographic bulge that altered society. As a group, they were the healthiest and wealthiest generation up to that time, and they were among the first to grow up genuinely expecting the world to improve with time.[6]

Baby Boomers' children are usually referred to as Generation X, or the Gen Xers. The birth years of this generation, is somewhat disputable but most agree that they were born between 1965 and 1984. One of the major trends for Gen Xers was that both parents worked outside the home. Consequently, many of this generation were latch-key kids who grew up pretty independently in nursery and after-school programs.

Growing up during a historical span of relative geopolitical peace for the United States, this generation saw the inception of the home computer, the rise of video games and cable television, and the development of the Internet as a tool for social and commercial purposes.

Gen Xers were often the children of parents separated by the increase in work-related travel and frequent geographic career moves. For instance, the father might have worked in Georgia while the mother remained with the children in their home state; or the father may have been a week-end dad and travelled throughout the week for his work. This put a heavy strain on couples and led to an increase in the divorce rate. Because, all too often they were the children of divorced parents, change was more the rule than the exception for Gen Xers.[7]

When it comes to their work environment, Gen Xers do not necessarily prefer social contact; in fact, many of the younger ones began the trend of working from different geographic locations or from home via computer (telecommuting). Hard work, for Gen Xers, means working alone, and being self-directed and self-sufficient. The eight-hour day is an anathema to some of them. Having no sense of a real start/stop time, Gen Xers work until they are done—or until the time zones complement the tasks that they must accomplish, which could mean the middle of the night. They run their children to and from numerous after-school activities, adjusting their schedules accordingly.

The Millennials, sometimes called the Generation Y (Gen Y), were born during a second baby boom that demographers locate disputably between 1984 and 2003. As such, members of this generation may be as young as seven and as old as twenty-six, with the largest slice still several years from adolescence. At 60 million strong, Gen Y is more than three times the size of Gen X; they're the biggest thing to hit the American scene since the 72 million Baby Boomers.[8] While most are still too young to make their mark or a name for themselves, nevertheless, they are a generation that must be reckoned with.

Our grandchildren belong to Gen Y. They respond to humor, irony, and the apparently unvarnished truth. They form a less homogenous market than their parents did. One factor contributing to this is their racial and ethnic diversity. Another is the fracturing of media, with network television having given way to a spectrum of cable channels, magazine goliaths, and the torrent of high-speed information from the Internet, YouTube, Facebook, and the like.

Along with cynicism, a distinctly practical worldview marks Gen Y, according to marketing experts.[9] Raised in dual-income, but frequently single-parent, families, they've been given considerable financial responsibility. Surveys show that they are deeply involved in family purchases, whether groceries, clothing, or more significant expenditures. Many will take on extensive debt to finance their college.

Gen Y people work very differently than previous generations. I have heard members of the Silent Generation say Gen Y kids don't have a work ethic. Actually, they do; it's just different. They love a lot of feedback and affirmation, and they multitask with ease. It is not unusual to see a Gen Y teen attending a meeting, with one eye on the speaker at the podium, while simultaneously texting on her cell phone. People in our grandchildren's Generation Y are not necessarily rule oriented, and older generations, like ours, misinterpret this as not having a work ethic. However, their work ethic is strong, it is just different.

This is one of the challenges that parenting grandparents must deal with as they raise their grandchildren. It is not so much a difference in values, but a difference in the behavioral and social ways in which Generation Y expresses those values that we, their grandparents, share with them.

One of our first reactions to the unfamiliar—that is, what we are not used to—is to judge it. Putting aside our judgments of and assumptions about today's world is important. When we criticize our current world, we are criticizing our grandchildren's world, and they already know and worry about insufficient energy resources, global warming, war, and terrorism. Also, criticism tends to make people, even young people, defensive; which, in turn, means that they will be more likely to respond with criticism. Criticism and defensiveness do not build bridges.

Instead, as grandparents, let's use our wisdom to help our grandchildren find value in each and every day of their lives. Let's find the goodness in life, so that we can help our kids balance the glaring negatives with some notable positives. All we have to do is look to those who volunteer their time to elevate the lives of those in need, both nationally and internationally. So many people of all ages and generations serve as volunteers. The Corporation for National and Community Service (CNCS), with headquarters in Washington, D.C., hosts many national volunteer programs, and also links with many nonprofits across the country to serve the needs of diverse communities. CNCS, in particular, offers some programs that provide financial stipends and education awards, which is the reason why it received this specific mention.

Why is this important for you and your grandchildren to know? First, it offers an opportunity for you and your grandchildren to serve others. Second, depending on the program, your grandchildren (age eighteen and older), or even you, can earn a $5,300-plus education award, making college or vocational school a reality. The Volunteers in Service to America (also known as AmeriCorps VISTA) is an AmeriCorps program focused exclusively on poverty. Those who join VISTA also receive a monthly stipend to serve for one year in communities across the United States in order to help the members of the community build their own capacity to eliminate poverty. (For more information, visit the CNCS website at www.nationalservice.gov.)

This is only one example. In truth, many positives exist in today's world, along with many problems that need resolution. This was true of our world also; even though the problems were different, they were no less serious.

When we embrace the goodness in the world, we bring people together, instead of driving them apart. One of the things I most love doing is asking children what people all over the world have in common. I recently asked a group of eight and nine-year-olds this question and their answers brought a smile to my face. One said, "we all lose our baby teeth; another, said we belong to families; a few said we all go to school, and one thought that surely children everywhere play hide and seek."

Interestingly, children find it much easier to answer this question than adults do. It makes for a great conversation around the dinner table, and it also makes us realize that we share many of the same values—regardless of which generation we belong to. Yes, we may express them differently, but the underpinnings remain the same.

Gentle Reminders

1. We assign high worth to our values. Let's make sure our grandchildren appreciate their roots and the family they belong to, because we all live our values and beliefs. When our values and behaviors align, we become strong role models for our grandchildren.

2. Values, while easily defined, find different forms of expression behaviorally, socially, and culturally. Let's

teach our grandchildren to appreciate both the similar and different ways in which we all express our values.

3. Grandparents' finest gift to their grandchildren is creating a safe environment in which they can express their hearts and share that expression out in the world. This teaches them not only that they belong to the world, but also that the world needs them.

4. Enjoy the generational differences between you and your grandchildren. Celebrate both the similarities *and* the differences. Talk about them together, and normalize them by removing judgment and criticism.

5. Goodness abounds in our world, as parenting grandparents talk about the beauty and love people share and experience, on a daily basis, whether locally, nationally, and/or internationally.

6. Visit the website, www.nationalservice.gov, for programs that give everyone (eighteen and older) an opportunity to be in service to others and to earn stipends and education awards in return. These stipends and education awards can be used to repay student loans and/or pay for college or vocational training.

PART III: SETTING BOUNDARIES FOR OUR GRANDCHILDREN BASED ON VALUES

We have looked at our grandkids' high-tech world and the ways in which we can best balance it with values and beliefs that support strong family relationships. In and of itself, nothing is "wrong" with the high-tech world. It provides many advantages, and it serves to make our lives easier in many ways if we choose to embrace it.

But, as with all things, technology must be utilized in an age-appropriate manner. That means setting some boundaries. The more we grandparents understand and learn about the incredible capabilities of the many varieties of technology available to our grandchildren, the more informed our decisions will be about the use of that technology and all the devices that are part of it.

Technology has changed our world, and it will continue to do so. Preventing the use of technology is as detrimental as allowing its overuse. As with any technological inventions—television, cell phones, gaming systems, MP3 players, smartphones, computers—time spent using the device or engaging with the technology must be balanced with time spent doing other things. People of all ages need mealtime, playtime, social time, quiet time, and so on.

When children and teens use technology excessively, that overuse isolates them. However, stopping them from using technology is not the answer; setting good boundaries and rules for usage is. Sometimes we ignore overuse because it cuts down on conflict; it creates a quiet household, and it gives everyone time to be alone.

One grandfather described his fourteen-year-old grandson, who would come home from school and head straight to his room, where he played computer games for hours. He even argued with his grandmother about having to come to the table for dinner. When, begrudgingly, he did come to the table, he ate quickly, and then returned to his room, having only minimal interaction and conversation with the family at the table.

Another grandparent described her fifteen-year-old granddaughter, who insisted that she needed a cell phone for safety reasons. Even though the expense strained the family's budget, the grandmother purchased a cell phone with texting options for her granddaughter. In the first month of usage, the granddaughter had more than 5,000 text messages. Along with the prohibitive costs, the granddaughter's grades in school started to drop, and her homework assignments were suddenly late or incomplete.

The problem here is not technology, but, rather, a lack of rules guiding the usage of technology and also a lack of clear expectations about usage. Priorities, even for teens, need to be set and observed, and when kids and teens don't respect the rules, they must accept the consequences. When we set boundaries, we teach our children about what we value and about what is important. They need to know that balancing all their activities—homework, family time, chores, time with friends, and computer/texting time—is more than an expectation; it is a family norm, and a requirement that they cannot ignore or be exempt from fulfilling.

Technology is not any different from the other things for which we set down rules and guidelines for our children and teens. We give them curfews, guidelines for doing their homework, and time frames for completing their chores; we scrutinize those with whom they can or cannot associate.

We need to have conversations with our grandchildren about reasonable expectations that reflect a balance between needs and wants. These expectations are rooted in what we value and believe is beneficial for their growth and maturity.

Today's children not only require reasonable expectations, they also need to understand the reasoning behind those expectations. The days when our parents told us "do it because I said so" are over. When we share our thoughts and reasons, we invite them to realize what is important to each of us. Dialogue allows our grandchildren to share their thoughts about what is important to them. This invests them in the decision-making process, and it is a tremendous opportunity for us to be positive role models by showing them how our decisions reflect what we value and believe.

One of the best ways to create harmony in a family is to do so around something everyone believes in and values. The more aligned our behaviors and decisions are with what we value, the more authentic we are. That's because what matters most will become a priority in our lives, and it will also offer us guidance on how we want to live, which is a very important lesson for our grandchildren to learn.

This is not to say that our grandchildren will always like our rules and expectations, and they will not always agree with them, either. They may, in fact, complain about being limited or not having the freedom that other kids they know have. This pushback is normal, especially during their teen years. (Chapter 4 addresses childhood and adolescent developmental phases, where we will explore all this further.)

Just remember that children of all ages respond better when offered a reason behind the decisions we make. As parenting grandparents, help your grandchildren understand your values and beliefs, and have discussions about why your values and beliefs are important to you. Let your grandchildren know that your values and beliefs guide your decisions; that way, you are a role model for them to emulate.

Gentle Reminders

1. Engage your grandchildren in discussions about values and beliefs on a regular basis. This will help define what is important and what matters in your family. It will also serve as the foundation for their own values and beliefs later in life.

2. Your values and beliefs offer a foundation for setting good and reasonable boundaries for your grandchildren. Values and beliefs also provide for meaningful family dialogue about what is important to the family and each of its members.

3. Dialogue also allows children to share their thoughts and beliefs. It sets the stage for understanding what is important, and why it is important.

4. Children of all ages respond better when offered a reason behind the decisions we make and the boundaries we set.

2
WHY ARE YOU SO OLD?

Grandparents interviewed across the country frequently indicated that their age was a frequent source of criticism from their grandchildren's peers. The reactions of both the grandparents and the grandchildren varied from not caring at all about this to feeling embarrassed and self-conscious.

As human beings, we hold certain conscious, or even unconscious, expectations related to life's cycles. For instance, years ago, women were in their late teens and twenties when they had babies. Many women today are in their thirties and forties when they have children. This is a result of many factors: more women go to college and graduate school; more women have professional careers following their education; the cost of living requires two income earners in many families; many men and women postpone marriage until they are in their thirties, and even older; many women desire to travel the world and/or even join service organizations, such as the Peace Corps and Volunteers in Service to America. These are but a few of the reasons why the birthing cycle has changed over the past twenty to fifty years.

The different ways in which we live our lives all have advantages and disadvantages. Each generation responds in its own way to external, societal influences in order to create new trends that are neither right nor wrong, neither good nor bad. As I like to say, "They are just so!"

Nevertheless, most people tend to judge that which is different, unfamiliar, and unusual. We scrutinize things which we know nothing about, and we act as if we have all the knowledge required to make an informed decision or conclusion. Unfortunately, ignorance—or a lack of information—does not stop people from labeling, criticizing, or offering opposing points of view that are negative. Children and teens can be quite sensitive to criticism and scrutiny, especially when these result from being "different"—whether that "difference" is real or imagined, they feel it, and so it is real to them. Very real.

As a parenting grandmother, if you have silver hair and wrinkles, you most likely will get some uninvited comments. As a parenting grandfather, if you are bald, slow-moving, and wrinkled, you will likely raise some curiosity, too. The words and actual phrasing might vary, but the essence of the question posed to you or your grandchildren is, "Why are your parents so old?" Don't dodge the comments or questions of your grandchildren's peers or their parents. Instead, think carefully about how you choose to handle and answer their inquiries.

First of all, realize that many children across the United States are in the same situation as your grandchildren: Their grandparents are raising them. This growing trend is making "parenting grandparents," also known as "kinship caregivers," much more commonplace.

As grandparents, we understand the value of open, honest, and direct conversations. Children are naturally good at this kind of conversation, provided that they receive encouragement to be respectfully open and direct. I encourage you to have this conversation at home with them, so that they are prepared if it comes up at school or any other venue where they might be with their peers. This is another opportunity to reinforce your values and beliefs, while simultaneously sharing your mutual feelings about what others might be saying or wondering about your elder status as a parent. When you share in this conversation, be as open as possible, and encourage your grandchildren to do the same.

There are significant advantages when you initiate this discussion with your grandkids where everyone shares candidly and honestly. First and foremost, you become a role model for them, showing them how to handle a sensitive, perhaps even difficult conversation. This is an exceptional communication skill for your grandchildren to acquire. Second and also important, you teach your grandchildren how to think in terms of options and choices. They will realize that more than one way to respond always exists in any situation. With your guidance, they will learn to find the response that will be both comfortable for and supportive of both them and you. This is another exceptional skill for them to develop.

Disregarding curious or critical comments only teaches children how to ignore or avoid problems, which is not a good life skill. It also prevents them from managing unsettling emotions, such as embarrassment, shame, sadness, anger, and others. Build your grandchildren's confidence and self-esteem by inviting them to share their thoughts and feelings about difficult issues, first with you and then with others.

One of the finest lessons a grandparent can teach a grandchild is how to be authentic. This means helping them to express, in both their words and behaviors, what they are feeling and thinking in a way that will allow the other person to hear and acknowledge them. When we say and do what is true for us, we reinforce our self-worth and self-esteem from the inside, and, as a result, we become far less dependent on the outside world to validate us. How fortunate is the grandchild who learns this lesson early in life.

Humor is another wonderful way to deal with the issue of a grandparent's age. Based on what I have learned from life as a parent and grandparent, I think the perfect age at which to have a child is fifty-five. Even though that is almost biologically impossible, it is the age at which we finally begin to figure things out. If only we had such wisdom at age twenty-five, thirty-five, or even forty-five! I know I would have spent a lot less time worrying about my children and a lot more time playing with them.

Play is so important to children. It is part of the definition of what it means to be a child. Don't miss this opportunity with your grandchildren. Along with giving our children a sense of safety, security, and belonging, we must also give them a sense of how important play, fun, and laughter are. Both your lives and theirs are filled with challenges and burdens, so find ways to make life lighter.

One of the most essential things we can teach our grandchildren is to learn what really matters in life. Help them to see that they can only find what really matters within themselves, not in the outside world. Help them to understand that your age does not really matter. All that really matters is how much you love them. As grandparents, we find a way of loving that escaped us as parents. We have the ability to love our grandchildren unconditionally, and that is magical for them and for us.

It's a pretty simple formula. It does not necessarily involve running our grandkids around after school for hours; it does not involve worrying about whether their grades will get them into college or vocational school, whether their teeth are straight, whether they are the best at what they do, or whether they have enough friends who won't pick on them or make them mad.

In some ways, elders have a serious advantage over younger parents. We may have a few more wrinkles, a head of silver hair or no hair at all, somewhat less energy, and a mind that is a bit more forgetful, but we do have wisdom and life experience. We also have hearts filled with compassion and love, and grandchildren are the fortunate recipients of these wonderful, hard-earned gifts.

One more important ingredient must go into the recipe for effectively answering the question, "Why are your parents so old?" That ingredient is attitude. The great part about attitude is that we each are the sole determiner of what our attitude will be in any given situation. Others can try to influence our attitude, but only we have the power to choose what our attitude—and our response—will be. We can either refuse or choose to allow the outside world to influence us. If we refuse, we offer ourselves the opportunity to tune in to inner guidance. Connecting with the inner self empowers us. Teaching our grandchildren how to connect with their own wise inner voice empowers them, too.

One of the things I admired most about my immigrant grandparents was how solid their attitudes about life were. Even when my grandmother told me how she and my grandfather lost their home during the Great Depression, she never conveyed a victimized or "poor me" attitude. My grandparents moved their family to a rental home, and then they repurchased their original home when economic conditions improved. I cannot remember a time when my grandparents were cynical about life and its challenges. They just always held this attitude of gratefulness for their life in America—for what living in America gave them. In both direct and subtle ways, they were constant mentors for me, even when I did not realize it.

The same is true for every parenting grandparent interviewed for this book. Although they face many challenges and difficulties as they try to raise their grandchildren, these grandparents never exhibited any pessimism or cynicism. Always be aware of what your attitude toward life is, as well as which values and beliefs provide the foundation for your attitudes. Clearly, your attitude influences your grandchildren, and you must know and remain aware of this. Be intentional about your attitude about life. When your grandkids are grown, they will reflect back and say, "My success as a person was birthed in my grandparents' positive, hopeful, and confident attitude toward life, despite their many challenges." (Remember the speech of that eighteen-year-old granddaughter in chapter 1.)

Gentle Reminders

1. Take advantage of the wisdom that comes with being a grandparent, and remember that it can only come with age and wrinkles.

2. Don't sidestep the difficult conversations about your being a "parenting grandparent" or "kinship caregiver." Embrace those conversations as opportunities to teach your grandkids values and beliefs.

3. Foster an environment where you and your grandchildren can be authentic and genuine; or, in their language, "real!"

4. Be open and direct when answering your grandkids' questions, and they will respect you for it; they will also learn to communicate the same way, with you and with others.

5. Be a role model of a positive, hopeful, and confident attitude, and your grandkids will internalize this in ways that will have deep meaning for them throughout their lives.

3
WHY AREN'T MY PARENTS RAISING ME?

PART I: THE DIFFICULT CONVERSATION

One of the important responsibilities you have as a parenting grandparent is to explain to your grandchildren why their parents are not raising them. Regardless of the reason why you are raising your grandchildren—their parents are in prison, struggling with addictions, too young and immature to raise a child, suffering from mental illness, dealing with a chronic or terminal illness, or have died—you need to have an age-appropriate conversation with your grandchildren to explain the reason to them. This conversation is absolutely necessary. This chapter will discuss the importance of telling grandchildren the truth in a way that they can understand, and it will also offer ways in which to help them manage their related emotions and ongoing reactions.

One in forty children in the United States has a parent in prison.[10] Research demonstrates that when their father is in prison, most children live with their mother. When their mother is in prison, many children live with their grandparents or other relatives.[11] This incarceration—of the grandparents' son or daughter, and the grandchildren's father and/or mother—is an overwhelming situation, for both the grandparents and the grandchildren. In addition, it is overwhelming on many levels: social, psychological, emotional, and financial.

When a parent goes to prison, children want to know what happened. It is best to tell them the truth. If you make up a story in an effort to protect your grandchildren, it could backfire and your grandchildren may feel deceived. In addition, you want your grandchildren to trust you, and the only way to learn trust is to experience it through honesty and telling the truth. Once again, how much you tell your grandchildren will depend on both their chronological and developmental age.

In addition, children have remarkable sensitivity, and so they may realize that you are hiding something from them. If they sense that you are withholding information, they are not apt to talk about their own worries and anxieties—and, even worse, they may imagine something far more terrible than what is actually happening.

This is a complicated situation, and it entails many challenges that you need to prepare for. Your grandchildren may hear rumors or gossip from neighbors or peers in the neighborhood or at school. If they hear the truth or a distortion of it from someone else, they may interpret that as meaning that they cannot talk to you about it. Even worse is the possibility that they may feel betrayed. The uneasiness created in children when they believe that they cannot talk openly or honestly leads to a barrier of mistrust in the relationship. Do not let half-truths or lies damage the trust your grandchildren have in you!

Because situations involving imprisonment can stir up feelings of shame, guilt, fear, sadness, and anger, children may be reluctant to talk to their teachers or peers. You may be the only one your grandchildren feel safe to talk with. Don't ruin their trust in you because of your own personal discomfort.

Children of incarcerated parents need stability in their lives. They need the truth told in a way that they can hear it with some degree of comfort, which means without judgment or anger.

For children age seven and younger, a simple explanation of what happened is sufficient, followed by assurances that you will care for and love them. Children in this age group may be satisfied with an explanation in which you simply tell them that Mom or Dad made a big mistake. Children of any age need predictability. They may want answers to any or all of these questions: "What is going to happen to me?" "Will I get to see my parent(s) or talk with them?" "How long will they be gone?" "Will they come back?" Whether or not young grandchildren ask these questions out loud, chances are good that they are thinking about them, as well as other questions.

Children age eight and older may want to know more details about what happened to their parents. They are old enough to understand that their parent(s) did something wrong and is being punished for it, and so their questions may be along these lines: "What exactly did my parent(s) do?" "Why did they do that if they knew it was wrong?" "What's going to happen?" You may need to provide them with more information than you did your younger grandkids. Older kids and teens also need the reassurance that you will love and care for them.

This is a difficult conversation to have with your grandchildren, no matter what ages they are. After all, it may be your son or daughter who is in prison. Even if it is your son- or daughter-in-law, you still will have your own emotional reaction to what is happening. Your feelings may range from anger to sorrow—and everything in between. How you handle your emotions will guide your grandchildren as to how they should manage theirs. It is essential that you be genuine and authentic when you discuss and express your feelings. Showing your vulnerability to your grandchildren gives them permission to express their own. Remember, you don't have to have all the answers, but you do need to be a good listener. Your grandkids will need a lot of reassurance at this time.

It is possible that not everyone in the family will agree on what to say to the children. As grandparents, let your inner wisdom help guide you and your family to reach a decision that is best for the children. Keeping secrets, gossiping, and criticizing will only inflame the situation and possibly contribute to a sense of shame and fear in your grandchildren. This is an opportunity to let your values and beliefs guide your responses during this difficult time. Of course, that teaches another important lesson for your grandchildren to learn how to do the same.

Your grandchildren will probably feel many conflicting emotions regarding the incarceration of their parent(s). Children and teens may feel angry and ashamed, yet they still may remain loyal to their parent(s). Keep in mind, your grandkids may be afraid that they will never see their parent(s) again. They may even fear that you will leave them, too.

Assuring your grandchildren that you love them and will not abandon them is the most important thing you can do. This assurance will help them feel more secure during this difficult and confusing time. Most important of all, keep the lines of communication open. Encourage your grandkids to express anything that troubles them, and they will begin to feel a sense of stability.

Your grandchildren's feelings may be different from yours, or they may be similar. Either way, listen when they want to talk about their parents. Their emotions may seem chaotic and unpredictable to you. Children and teens in this situation may want their parents one day; but, the next day, the kids may not want to have anything to do with their parents. It is natural for your grandchildren to miss their parents, yet be very angry and even ashamed.

Sometimes we don't know what to say, especially to young children. This is why listening is so important. If you listen carefully to your grandchildren's words, you will hear what they need from you. Some children may be very timid and reserved in their responses, while others may openly express fear, resentment, and other emotions. As you listen, affirm that you understand their feelings, however confusing they may seem. You don't have to try to change their feelings or make them go away. More than ever, your clear communication of stability, safety, and unconditional love is essential to your grandchildren. Strong emotions, combined with confusion, require that your words and behavior show your grandchildren that they are safe and loved. Safety includes their feeling that they are free to express whatever is going on inside them.

When life gets chaotic, one of the best things we can do is establish a routine. Doing this enables us to give our grandchildren a sense of predictability, which, in turn, will help them feel more secure; it also shows them that you have things under control. At first, they may balk at the structure you are offering and insisting upon, but, in time, it will provide support and reassurance—for them and also for you.

Be aware that this time will be especially difficult if you are experiencing anger toward your adult child and want no contact with him or her. Your grandchildren, on the other hand, may be missing their parent(s) and wanting to see them. Just remember this: You do not need to feel or want the same things that your grandchildren do, but you do need to acknowledge and respect their feelings and wants.

If you are struggling with your own emotions and feeling overwhelmed, be sure you get the support you need and deserve. During this challenging time, it might be very helpful for you to talk to someone you can trust and feel comfortable with, whether it be a sibling, friend, religious adviser, grandparent support group, or counselor. Seeking guidance will also allow you to talk with someone about managing your grandchildren's complex responses. Most important, know that you are not alone; people, professionals, and organizations can help, but you have to reach out for that help.

Siblings respond very differently to stress, and this may contribute to your grandchildren's challenges. Some children and teens become talkative; others become silent. Some may become clingy and need a lot of reassurance; others pull away and keep to themselves. Some may act as if nothing is bothering them; others act out and misbehave. As parenting grandparents, you will have to adjust to a variety of your grandchildren's emotional responses, some of which will be easier for you to handle than others. That is why support for you during this period is so very important.

Let's take a look at some appropriate responses we might utilize to deal with our grandchildren, depending on their ages and personalities.

<u>Nonverbal Children and Teens</u>

Some children, like some adults, may find it impossible to share their deep emotions. Specifically, as related to the absence of parents who have been imprisoned, feelings of shame, fear, guilt, confusion, anger (even rage), rejection, or abandonment may be overwhelming your grandchildren, but they may not be able to put their feelings into words.

Some children and teens may be introverted by nature, which simply means that they need to process their thoughts and feelings internally and alone. They may also have distancing tendencies, which means that the more you move toward them, the more they move away—physically, socially, psychologically, and emotionally. Do not take these responses personally, as they are your grandchildren's unique way of coping.

As grandparents, try not to make nonverbal children's or teens' responses "wrong" or "bad." Instead, try to keep judgment out of your responses as much as possible. Accepting your grandchildren's responses helps them experience us as more trustworthy, which, in turn, helps them feel safer and more secure. Avoiding judgment also communicates that you understand your grandchild's responses, and this is vital during such a difficult time.

Here are several different ways to communicate with nonverbal children and teens:

- Verbalize some of the emotions that might be typical for children/teens who have incarcerated parents. This approach "normalizes" children's and teens' feelings.

  You could make a statement, such as: "I would understand it if you are feeling sad and afraid. If you decide you want to talk about your thoughts or feelings, I am ready to listen."

Even if your grandchildren do not acknowledge feeling this way, you are reassuring them that it is okay to have these emotions. If they deny feeling this way, you can gently tell them what you are observing that concerns you.

- Describe what you notice about your grandchildren's behavior or mood that might be new or different. Feel free to ask if what you observe is a sign that they are experiencing difficult emotions. "I notice that you are having trouble falling asleep (or "are having more nightmares", or "are having trouble concentrating") lately. This is unusual for you. I am concerned that you are really upset right now about what is happening to your mom (or "dad")."

If your grandchildren affirm upset feelings or thoughts, invite them to talk about these with you whenever they are ready. They can also write about or draw how they are feeling. Also important is your willingness to acknowledge that you are upset, too, and that you understand how hard it is to deal with these feelings. Don't go into great detail about your emotions; simply acknowledging that you are experiencing distress normalizes their own emotions.

- If your grandchildren demonstrate unusual and atypical behaviors or moods for a prolonged period of time, they may need the counseling of a child or adolescent social worker or psychologist. This counselor may offer art therapy, play therapy, or another form of therapy that will encourage the expression of their troubling emotions or thoughts. These therapists will also offer you guidance to help you support and deal with your grandchildren's mental, emotional, and behavioral challenges during this difficult time.

Acting-Out Children and Teens

Children and teens who misbehave, or "act out," their crushing thoughts and emotions are generally communicating that they have an inability to manage overwhelming impulses in constructive ways. Their anger, rage, fear, shame, and devastating thoughts may be manifested in self-destructive behaviors.

Your grandchildren, whether younger kids or teens, may skip school, get into fights with peers, be more verbally argumentative, display attitudes that are contemptuous, and/or become aloof from family and friends. Excessive eating (or refusing to eat), mood swings, temper tantrums, crying, fighting, and arguing are but a few of the behaviors that they might display. Where teens are concerned, be aware of the use of alcohol or drugs. This can occur with younger kids, too, so if you see signs that concern you, don't ignore them!

Grandparents who observe such acting-out behaviors need to realize that deep psychological and emotional impetus motivate these aberrant behaviors. These behaviors may be frightening to both your grandchild and to you. Some effective and beneficial parenting-grandparent responses might include:

- Sitting down with your grandchildren and sharing in a concerned way, but without judgment, the behaviors you are observing. By affirming what a painful and difficult period this is for them, you can also indicate that both acceptable and unacceptable ways to manage their thoughts and emotions exist. "Anything that ultimately hurts you or someone else is not okay. I understand you are hurting, so let's figure out ways for you to express those feelings and deal with them better."

- Here are some things you can ask your older grandchildren: "What do you need from me right now?" "What are you most afraid of right now?" "What is making you especially angry right now?" "One of the hardest things to talk about is shame. Are you experiencing feelings of shame or embarrassment right now?" "How can I best help and support you right now?"

Your grandchildren may or may not respond to your questions, but they will certainly get the message that you are tuned in, that you care, and that you are someone who is safe to talk to about their deep hurt. Never diminish your influence by their outward response. Speak to their mind and heart, regardless of how they respond.

You might encourage children age ten and older to write down their thoughts and feelings, perhaps even write a letter to their parents (though this letter may or may not ever be sent). The idea is to give them a safe way to express their inner feelings. For children who don't want to write, suggest drawing, painting, or using puppets as a means to create the outer dialogue (expression) of their internal emotions.

Another successful technique includes the use of color. Talking through metaphor may help your grandchildren feel a bit more distant from the pain they may be feeling. Ask, "If you could give a color to your throat right now, what would it be?" "How about your heart, what color is it right now?" "How about your tummy, what color is it?"

When children answer "black" or "brown," you can ask them: "What is making your heart feel so black?" "When did this start?" "What color would you like it to be?" "How can we help it be that color?" (Chapter 7 explains this technique in greater detail.)

Children younger than ten might need your encouragement to verbalize their feelings, so that they do not misbehave or act out. When you notice your grandchildren behaviorally expressing frustration, encourage them by saying: "Use your words instead of kicking the furniture." "How about if both of us take a time-out so that we can sit down and talk with each other? I want to listen to what you're thinking and feeling right now."

If you use either of these statements, be sure there are no distractions. Shut off the television and/or computer, stop whatever you are doing, and let the kids know that you are ready to give them your undivided attention. If others are around, create a quiet, private space for you and your grandchildren to have your conversation.

Children and Teens Who Act as If Nothing Is Wrong

When children and teens act as if nothing has happened—or if they seem to be coping well with the short- or long-term incarceration of one or both parents—they need to be observed even more closely. Be cautious about assuming that they really are coping well. Some children or teens may have delayed reactions; others may bury their emotions and disconnect from them. Some, not knowing how to react, may just pretend that they are fine. Be sure to make yourself available to your grandchildren. Also, be sure to give them permission, by both your words and your behavior, to experience their thoughts and emotions. You need to show that you are comfortable with their doing so, and you can make a statement, such as: "You seem to be okay, but I want you to know it's okay if you feel angry, sad, or fearful, or if you have any other feelings related to what has happened to your parents." Remain available to hear their response to this, which may come forth immediately or after a period of time.

Again, give your grandchildren permission to express any painful feelings or thoughts they may be experiencing. You don't have to "fix" their pain; but, as their grandparent, you can acknowledge it and help them experience their true emotions and thoughts in a safe, accepting environment. Let your grandkids know how much you care about them and love them—and that you will continue to love them, even if they express strong emotions. Good listening skills and the ability to communicate understanding are key responses to children and teens struggling with difficult emotions.

Gentle Reminders

1. Children (younger kids and teens, alike) of incarcerated parents need stability in their lives. They need to hear the truth in an age-appropriate way, but without judgment.

2. Affirming your grandchildren's feelings, and reassuring them that you love and will care for them, is very important during such a difficult time—no matter how old they are.

3. Be aware of your own needs, too, during this difficult time. Make it okay to seek support for yourself, and also for your grandchildren, if necessary. Parenting-grandparent groups are a wonderful way to receive the understanding, support, and help you need. Some of these groups even have teen support groups, so be sure to inquire.

PART II: CONTACT OR NO CONTACT WITH THE JAILED PARENT?

One of the biggest decisions parenting grandparents face as a result of the incarceration of their adult child (or in-law) is whether it is in their grandchildren's best interest to stay in touch with or visit their parents. Some of the things needing consideration when making this difficult decision include:

- nature of the previous relationship with the parent

- history of parental abuse, neglect, and/or abandonment

- what helps your grandchildren feel more secure and safe

If your grandchildren's previous relationship with their parents was combative, unstable, abusive, or neglectful, do not pressure your grandchildren to visit, write, or call their parents. Seek professional counseling if this is your situation. Abuse, neglect, and abandonment are complex issues that leave deep scars. You do not want to create additional strain or stress on an already dysfunctional relationship; you do want to ensure the safety and security of your grandchildren.

In cases where the previous relationship between parents and children was stable and loving, contact with the jailed parents may be in your grandchildren's best interest. It may help teens or younger kids come to terms with what led to the incarceration, and it may help the family stay connected. This may also help all the family members adjust to what has happened, both during and after the parents' release from jail.

Studies show that, when parents and children have had a positive relationship, children do better at home if they can visit the parents in jail. Children usually think and worry that prison conditions are much worse than they really are. Seeing the parent(s) in prison can ease the minds of children and teens. Several organizations sponsor programs that make it easier for children to visit their parents in prison.[12] Find out whether the prison in your situation has such programs.

Taking your grandchildren to visit their parents in prison may not be practical in terms of distance, cost, or both. Consider other options until you are able to make the prison visit. Telephone calls, letters, and sending copies of report cards and school papers, along with greeting cards, are but a few ways your grandchildren can stay in touch with their jailed parents. Some prisons also allow computer time to inmates; you can investigate this option, too.

PART III: MY ADULT CHILD IS IN JAIL

Up to this point, the chapter has focused on your grandchildren's reactions to the incarceration of one or both of their parents. The grandparents interviewed shared moving stories about the deep sorrow they carried as a result of their adult child's imprisonment, while simultaneously trying to cope with daily life and the issues related to raising their grandchildren.

> *Wayne and Sheree were on their first vacation since retiring from their careers. For a long time, their dream had been to visit Jamaica, the place where Sheree was born and had lived until she was eight years old. On the third day of their vacation, Wayne received a call from Child Protective Services. Wayne and Sheree's son was in jail, arrested for larceny. If Wayne and Sheree did not return immediately, their grandchildren would be placed in foster care.*
>
> *Wayne and Sheree were in shock, as their son had no previous criminal record. Their son's wife had abandoned her husband and their two sons four months earlier. Wayne was tearful as he said, "What were we to do? We could not let our grandboys be put into foster care, yet we did not want to come home. It felt selfish, but this was the trip of our dreams."*

Wayne and Sheree's experience is not atypical. All too often, grandparents must give up their dreams, their retirement, their lifestyle, and their 401(k) plans (or other savings) in order to raise their grandchildren—because their own adult children are not willing to fulfill that responsibility or simply cannot for various reasons. The inner conflict overwhelms these grandparents, yet their deep devotion to and love for their grandchildren leads them to let go of the life they have earned and dreamed of. They return to the role of "parent" again—this time, as parenting grandparents—and take on all the sacrifices and demands that parenting entails.

Other grandparents interviewed spoke about their adult children's war with alcohol and drugs. Many shared how their adult sons or daughters, unable to break the habit, resorted to criminal acts in order to support their addictions. Many children born to addicted parents wrestle with codependent behaviors. These lead to push-and-pull (chapter 6 offers examples) relationships that breed mistrust and a neediness that tarnishes the children's self-worth and puts them at risk for a troubled future.

Still other grandparents interviewed spoke with heavy hearts about a particular child, from amongst their three, four, or five children, who struggled from early childhood with feelings of alienation, low self-worth, and internal conflicts. These children just seemed "different," and their internal struggle too frequently led them astray and into criminal activities. (Chapter 8 includes an adult child's story in order to help us better understand the inner world of these conflicted individuals.)

Grandparents whose adult children have a criminal history are frequently criticized by legal systems, social systems, educators, and peers for not having raised their now-adult child very well. Some further argue that these grandparents will not be able, and should not be allowed, to parent their grandchildren, given their parenting history with their own child.

This criticism weighs heavily on grandparents. They are often made to feel like failures, despite having raised their other adult children quite successfully. They become very upset with judges, case workers, and lawyers during the course of defending themselves and trying to prove that they are capable of, and suitable for, raising their grandchildren.

This happens with enough regularity that many of the grandparents interviewed verbalized how reluctant they are to contact social-service agencies for fear that their grandchildren will be taken from them. Nevertheless, grandparents are desperate for the financial, legal, and social programs these agencies offer to help them better raise their grandchildren.

Given the many stressors these grandparents carry, it would be understandable if you felt overwhelmed by the complexity of raising your grandchildren. It would also be easy for your distress to leak into your conversations and interactions with your grandchildren. It is very important for you, as parenting grandparents, to find within yourselves the ability to temper your internal reactions, so that your opinions, biases, fears, and strong emotions do not negatively color the conversations or relationship between you and your grandchildren.

This is an exacting expectation to hold for anyone, let alone grandparents who did not ask for this responsibility and who, whether suddenly or over time, found your lives had become unpredictable, and filled with enormous change and complex challenges. So many stressors and pressures lay on your shoulders as parenting grandparents. Your ability to be sensitive to your grandchildren's needs, to be a good listener, and to provide a safe and secure home for them while managing your own deep anxieties and concerns is exactly what makes raising your grandchildren both noble and sacred work.

Gentle Reminders

1. Base your decision on whether your grandchildren will be in contact with and/or see their incarcerated parent on the nature of their previous relationship. If a history of abuse, neglect, or abandonment exists, seek professional counseling to make the best decision.

2. Parenting grandparents face many stressors as they begin to raise their grandchildren. Don't allow yourself to reach an overwhelmed state before seeking guidance and support.

3. It is the formidable challenges that you face as parenting grandparents, and your willingness to deal with them, that make your commitment to raising your grandchildren such noble and sacred work.

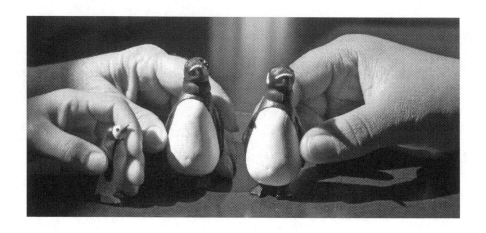

4
THE DEVELOPMENTAL STAIRCASE

PART I: TRYING TO UNDERSTAND THE WORLD

The previous chapter began to explore the ways in which your grandchildren's chronological ages influence how much you might share with them about what happened to their parents, as well as why you are now raising them. *Chronological age* is measured in years, beginning with our date of birth. Another measure of our age is *developmental age*; this is different from chronological age, and it is measured in stages.

The *developmental stages* are the expected and sequential order by which we develop life skills. It begins at infancy and continues through old age. For example, developmentally, a baby crawls before he stands, and he stands before he walks. On a psychological and emotional developmental level, in order to learn to trust other people, an infant must bond with and trust his initial caregiver.

As children, teens, and adults move through the developmental stages of life, they need to achieve and accomplish developmental milestones. For instance, in the first year of life, a baby learns to roll over, crawl, walk, and talk (even if this is only making sounds and/or attempting to form words). Certain milestones are expected to be achieved within each unique developmental stage. These stages apply to us throughout our life cycle on several levels—physical, emotional, mental, and social. Our ability to traverse these stages determines so many aspects of our life as we grow. For instance, our success—or failure—during any of these developmental stages, in turn, influences our level of maturity, the quality of our relationships, our ability to take risks, the decisions we make, our self-esteem, our sense of self-worth, and more.

Reviewing the developmental stages will give some context for understanding your grandchildren's behaviors, emotional responses, and perhaps any developmental delays or regressions that may have occurred as a result of loss or trauma. It will also help you determine what you can realistically expect from your grandkids.

So much of our ability to pass through these stages depends on our environmental circumstances, as well as the amount of nurturing we do or do not receive as a newborn, and throughout our growing-up years. Also, we will pay attention to significant losses, illnesses, and traumas, which can interrupt our ability to navigate a particular developmental stage successfully. Since many of your grandchildren have experienced interrupted relationships with their parents for a variety of reasons, this will give us a good foundation on which to understand what is going on with them, and it will also offer some guidance on how to manage their challenges.

The information presented is based on the Eight Stages of Development, developed by psychiatrist Erik Erikson in 1956. According to Erikson, the socialization process of human beings consists of eight stages or crises.[13] His Eight Stages of Development were formulated not through experimental work, but through wide-ranging experience in psychotherapy, including extensive experience with children and adolescents from a variety of social classes.

Erikson regarded each stage as a "psychosocial crisis," which arises and demands resolution before the next stage can be satisfactorily negotiated. Just as the foundation of an apartment building is essential to the floors above it, mastery of the first developmental stage is essential if the child is to manage the next and subsequent stages satisfactorily. It is important to note that the stages can overlap. Any or all of them may have approximate beginning and end points, depending on the uniqueness of each child's psychosocial growth or challenges.

This text highlights the significance of each of Erikson's stages. Part I focuses on stages 1 through 4; part II, on stages 5 through 7. (Part I of chapter 5 focuses on stage 8, which is the latter part of life). Following this explanation of the stages, some of the stories shared by the grandparents interviewed will further underscore how significant these developmental stages are.

Stage 1: Learning Basic Trust versus Basic Mistrust

Chronologically, this is the period of infancy through the first one or two years of life. Children, when nurtured and loved, develop the ability to trust, as well as a sense of security and optimism toward life. When their parents present consistent, adequate nurturing and care, children develop basic trust, realizing that people are dependable and the world can be a safe place.

In this stage, children learn how to express what they need, accept nurturing, and bond with the parents or grandparents who love with cheerfulness and smiles. As trust in the external world builds, children develop a healthy dependence and show signs of engaging with life. Moving through this first stage successfully means the children have a strong foundation of trust and security in life; as a result, these children are able to move successfully through future developmental stages.

If your grandchildren missed the essential attachment period during this first stage, you may notice behaviors that are of concern, such as constant crying, interrupted sleep, poor appetite, fear of being alone, an inability to be soothed, and so on. The inability to bond physically and emotionally because of frustrated, unmet dependency needs weakens the foundation that children need in order to navigate subsequent developmental stages.

As these children grow, a deep sense of mistrust about life develops within them; they may be afraid to ask for what they need, and they may not even be aware of what they need. Furthermore, these children may experience a feeling of emptiness as they grow; not surprisingly, as adolescents and even as adults, they become prone to developing addictions to food, tobacco, drugs, alcohol, and so on.

During this critical stage, as parenting grandparents you must seek to help your grandchildren trust you; you can do this by making sure that they feel a sense of security in your presence. Infants or one-year-olds who experience trauma during this tender phase of life might end up struggling with anxiety about their needs not being met. By creating an environment that offers consistency, nurturing, predictability, and safety, grandparents have a unique opportunity to prevent their grandchildren's experiencing prolonged mistrust of people and life. Thus, this crucial stage demands vigilant attention.

> *Michael is an eleven-year-old whom I have seen in my private practice for about six years now. His grandmother brought him to me because he was so overcome with fear that he could not go to the bathroom alone during the daytime, let alone at night. In fact, at night, Michael slept with either his grandmother or grandfather, both of whom have not slept together in a long time. Michael struggles with the basic issue of not trusting his external environment sufficiently to feel safe and secure.*

> *He also does not have within him the resources to trust that he can manage his fears and keep himself safe. Michael struggles with the psychological and emotional challenges of learning to trust, which has interrupted his ability to develop a sense of autonomy and initiative, challenges which occur in the second and third developmental stages.*

> *Michael was in an orphanage in another country when he was adopted at age four. His American adoptive parents subsequently divorced, and his father remarried and lives in another state. His mother lives with her parents (Michael's grandparents). She is a nurse who works the midnight shift, so his grandparents must take on much of the responsibility for parenting Michael.*

Michael has experienced significant fear, which immobilizes him both day and night. He displays a lot of fear and anxiety associated with early abandonment. His own goal in therapy is to be able to have one friend and not be so scared.

At age eleven, Michael, developmentally, should be well past issues of separation and autonomy. This is the important thing to remember with children who have had early trauma and post-traumatic stress: Chronologically, they are one age; but, psychologically, emotionally, and socially, they are far younger. In fact, Michael struggles with developmental issues of children who are three to five years old.

Hopefully, this will help us understand why some grandchildren act younger than their chronological age.. It would be easy for Michael's grandparents to say to him, "You are too old to be afraid to go to the bathroom by yourself, and certainly too old to need one of us to sleep with you." But, the fact is, Michael is far younger emotionally and mentally than his chronological age of eleven. This is because of the trauma of abandonment that he experienced as an infant and toddler in the orphanage, which he later re-experienced when his adoptive father left after the divorce.

Hypnotherapy has worked very well with Michael, as he responds to the subconscious, corrective suggestions that build his confidence and help him better manage old fears and anxieties. This approach helps build the psycho-emotional foundation that Michael never had as a result of his abandonment by his biological parents, which resulted in his placement in an orphanage.

Over the last year, Michael has made significant progress. With his circle of support and nurturing—the most important of which are his grandparents and mother—Michael now is able to go to the bathroom alone, and he is also able to sleep alone in his bedroom.

Children are incredibly resilient, but those who have deep-seated trauma require a good deal of patience and understanding from the adults in their lives—parents and grandparents, as well as the professionals who work with these children. Again, the intention of this information is to assist you, as parenting grandparents, helping you understand that your grandchildren's chronological age and developmental age may differ, often significantly. The many parenting grandparents interviewed related stories that centered around the themes of abandonment, abuse, and neglect. These experiences devastate children of any age. However, the younger the children are when these issues occur, the fewer internal resources they have to cope with such trauma.

Because of this, helping your grandchildren handle the difficult consequences of abuse, neglect, and abandonment requires multiple resources. It is important to seek professionals who have expertise in Post-Traumatic Stress Disorders (PTSDs), because such experts can better help your grandchildren cope with the negative impact these experiences have had on their mental, psychological, emotional, and social growth. Nevertheless, no professionals or resources can be a substitute for the unconditional love and understanding that you provide to your grandchildren on a daily basis.

Stage 2: Learning Autonomy versus Shame

This stage begins when children are about two years old and lasts through the age of three and a half or four. Well-parented children emerge from this stage sure of themselves, elated with their newfound control, and feeling pride rather than shame. Children at this age are known for their strong will, temper tantrums, and stubbornness. After all, they are trying to develop autonomy or a certain amount of self-sufficiency and independence. For example, they may resolutely fold their arms, not wanting to hold your hand when it's time to cross the street. The sound of "no" begins to echo through the house, the playground, or the supermarket.

> *While interviewing one parenting grandmother, her two-year-old granddaughter became bored, tired of waiting for her grandma to finish the conversation with me. Deciding that I was the villain, the*

child pointed her finger at me, locked a look of certainty on her face, and boldly told me, "Go away!" It was hard not to laugh, but this is typical of toddlers exploring their independence and autonomy.

When that did not work, she commanded, "Don't look at me!" One way or another, she was going to make me disappear. This is also pretty typical of toddlers as they move through this developmental stage, so keep your sense of humor and enjoy their creative ways of expressing their "power."

During this second developmental stage, toddlers should gain more control over their own bodies, acquiring new mental and verbal skills, and learning right from wrong. As a parenting grandparent, guide your grandchildren gradually, yet firmly; praise and accept their attempts to be independent, and their autonomy will develop.

It is during this stage that you, as parenting grandparents, have the opportunity to support your grandchildren's ability to build their self-esteem and sense of autonomy. This stage becomes the foundation for later traits, such as determination, self-reliance, motivation, and self-confidence. If you are too permissive, too harsh, and/or too demanding, toddlers can feel defeated, and then they may experience excessive shame and doubt. When this happens, growing children's continued attempts to regain feelings of control, power, and competency may fail.

In terms of attitudes and behaviors, toddlers may become very controlling and can appear to be quite overconfident. Alternatively, toddlers may do the opposite, becoming overly timid, self-doubting, and indecisive. Whether children become too aggressive or too passive, they suffer from poor personal boundaries and a sense of powerlessness.

Any children who experience trauma at this tender age may well struggle with abandonment issues, shame, and a need for control. This need to control their world is an attempt to constrict it, or make it smaller, so that these children can feel safer. Oftentimes, regardless of age, individuals who have a high need to control life really have a high need for safety and security. In essence, they are saying, "I can trust myself more than I can trust the external world."

This second developmental stage is critical because it provides the underpinnings for the development of self-esteem. How we handle our toddlers during this stage can make these children permanently shameful or permanently empowered. Our little ones are cataloging images that will influence them for a long time. If we are too permissive, it plants the seed of conceit, which will likely result in their becoming egotistical. If we discipline them in a way that makes them feel ashamed, they then may struggle with an ever-present need to avoid other people, thinking that, if they are not close to others, no one will see their shame. Invisibility and avoidance become the defense against feelings of shame and self-doubt.

During this stage, many toddlers successfully accomplish toilet training, which requires a giving of their will. While no area of development should involve forcing or rushing children, this one, in particular, should not. Simply put, you cannot "make" your grandchildren use the potty. Many children will withhold if forced or rushed before they are ready for toiled training, and this can lead to problems with constipation. Shame should never be a part of toilet training, because it can lead to issues of shame and hiding in other aspects of life as these children grow. Toilet training can become a "war" between parenting grandparents and their grandchildren. You can prevent this by determining whether your grandchildren are chronologically and developmentally ready for toilet training. In other words, children who are physically ready but emotionally immature might have greater success a bit later on; if this describes your situation, you might consider postponing toilet training for a while.

Casey is almost four years old but not yet toilet-trained. His grandmother, Sophia, is frustrated because it is expensive to buy pull-up diapers, and the other kids his age frequently tease Casey, causing him to withdraw from playing with them. Casey disappears to another room when he has to have a bowel movement. When his grandma finds him, she calls him "willful," and this triggers a pattern of tears and yelling from Casey. Sophia described herself as being at her wit's end.

Holding his bowel movements has made going to the bathroom painful for Casey. This, plus his grandmother's criticism, has contributed to a toilet-training crisis for Casey. When I saw Casey in treatment, it became clear that he had no investment in his potty chair. Sophia and I talked about options that might help Casey feel that he had some choices regarding his own toilet training.

Sophia took Casey to a store to buy an attachment that would fit the adult toilet seat in her home. Sophia let Casey choose the toilet seat he wanted, and he helped her attach it when they got home. He loved that his favorite cartoon character decorated his special seat. Casey also felt proud that he could sit on the big toilet. Sophia also bought Casey a DVD about toilet training. This video featured another one of his favorite cartoon characters, which served to normalize the whole effort.

In the meantime, Casey's two ten-year-old cousins both encouraged him, showing him how to use the toilet to urinate. This became a game for Casey, and he loved being a "big boy" like his cousins. Along with this, Sophia gave her grandson a lot of praise and encouragement, plus a lot of reassurance.

The absence of a father figure was hard on Casey, especially when it came to something as intimate as toilet training. Parenting grandparents who are single may have to do some compensating depending on the gender of the grandchildren.

Casey was physically ready, but, emotionally, he had been overwhelmed ever since his mother was sent to jail for selling drugs. Living with his grandmother provided Casey with love and stability, but it did not erase the abandonment he felt when his mother suddenly disappeared.

Children, regardless of age, feel internal confusion, fear, and anxiety as a result of the sudden absence of a parent. Actually, such absences also affect adults, but we have the internal resources necessary to help us cope with such circumstances; children, however, have not yet acquired these resources.

Several things can help children through this developmental transition, such as establishing daily, predictable routines; offering suitable, age-appropriate explanations; and providing a good deal of reassurance that they are safe and loved. Trying new things, teaching new behaviors, or supporting the development of new skills are not the most important issues during times of crisis and instability. Managing your grandchildren's emotional and psychological world is the highest priority during such a period.

In general, during this second developmental stage, finding a disciplinary balance is important. You should give toddlers choices, but these choices should be limited to those that you, as the parenting grandparent, can live with. It's important to give time-outs and set limits, rather than default to shouting or spanking. When disciplining, it's also important to separate your love for the children from their behavior. For example, you can let your grandchildren know, "I love you, but I do not like it when you run away from me near a busy street." You also can provide alternatives: "No, you cannot play with the TV remote, but you can play with some of my old pots or pans."

Finally, keep in mind that discipline needs to be consistent. If you say you are going to do something, do it. Otherwise, your grandchild will learn to ignore your disciplinary techniques as nothing more than meaningless threats.

Stage 3: Learning Initiative versus Guilt

This stage occurs between the ages of four to six. Sometimes this is referred to as "play" age, because children play imaginative games and engage in a considerable amount of fantasy and pretend. They have learned to cooperate with each other, and they may take turns leading and following. If we understand and support children's efforts to demonstrate initiative, they will develop a sense of purpose and importance. The voice inside them says, "I matter, and I can do important things."

The purpose of this stage is to develop an identity that is separate from the identities of others. In the process, children acquire knowledge about the world, and also about their bodies, social groups, and gender roles. In this developmental stage, young children realize that behaviors have consequences and so they learn what they can and cannot do. They also learn what they do and do not have the power to change or control.

It is not unusual during this stage to hear some "pearls of wisdom" from your grandchildren. For instance, I am inexplicably and irrationally afraid of cats. My grandson, six at the time, appointed himself my "protector." When one of his cats began to circle me, and I became very anxious, he picked up the cat and took him outside. When he returned to the room, he sat down beside me, looked at me and said, "Don't be afraid, Grandmom. It's just about love. That's all it is, just about love." My grandson was right, and he still is—whether in regard to grandchildren or other family members, people in general, or pets, life is about love.

During this developmental stage, the receiving of approval becomes very important. If children do not get the approval they need to develop a healthy ego, they become starved for it, and, as a result, they display a lot of neediness. They either become willing to do anything just to get attention and approval, or they may try to overpower peers and siblings in abusive ways. Either way, these children are struggling with feelings of powerlessness.

It is vital that you, as parenting grandparents, help your grandchildren experience being "in charge" in little ways. Too much initiative without a sense of guilt can lead to ruthlessness—that is, not caring who gets hurt in the process of achieving one's own desires. On the other hand, too much guilt can lead children to be overly cautious, burdened by a sense of being "bad," which will cause them to feel guilty. Children immobilized by guilt remain unduly dependent on adults, do not really feel accepted by peer groups, and have restricted play and imagination. Therefore, children punished for attempting to show initiative are likely to develop feelings of guilt, which, in excess, will lead to unhealthy inhibition.

Five-year-old Lakesha is the oldest of three siblings. Her parents married after her birth, and their relationship is best described as argumentative and abusive. With both her parents addicted to alcohol, Lakesha's home environment is unstable, unpredictable, and chaotic.

Lakesha's grandparents, Sadie and Willie, babysit her in their home every day. Over the last several months, Sadie said her granddaughter has been complaining of stomachaches. She also has learned that Lakesha's sleep is erratic at night, and she is becoming more timid and fearful on a daily basis. She engages in a lot of pleasing behaviors, seems anxious about playing with neighborhood children, and has developed rashes on her hands and feet and behind her knees.

Lakesha told Sadie that she is afraid because her parents are always yelling and screaming at each other. Lakesha further described that she feels like she is the cause of her parents' arguments, so she has been trying not to make any mistakes so that her parents won't get upset. Even when her younger siblings disturbed her toys, she would "hide" her upset so that her parents would not get mad at her, her siblings, or each other. Sadie said it seemed as if Lakesha were walking on eggshells at home, even though the child was only five years old. On some level, Lakesha had concluded that if she were "really good," her parents would stop arguing and stay together.

This is an unrealistic burden for a five-year-old to carry. But her fear of abandonment contributed to Lakesha's grandiose sense of being able to keep her parents from divorcing. Her thoughts might have gone something like this, "If I am *really good,* my parents won't argue and won't leave us." Again, we see the effect of the fear of abandonment on young children. The reality is that Lakesha's parents' problems are unrelated to her, and they did divorce, despite the guilt and anxiety that she internalized, as well as her attempts to be "perfect" or "really good."

The more Lakesha would strive to please her parents, the more she disconnected from her own needs—and the less likely it became that she would be able to satisfy her own needs (as much as she could at her age) or to accept nurturing from the stable, loving adults in her life. Essential to growing self-confidence and self-esteem is feedback that offers approval, recognition, and reassurance that we are loved and wanted—regardless of whether we make mistakes or not. Lakesha's grandparents need to offer her a secure environment, along with the message that it is okay to make mistakes. Lakesha needs a lot of reassurance that she is loved and wanted just the way she is.

It is impossible for children to achieve autonomy when they must constantly walk on eggshells in order to keep peace in their home, especially when they blame themselves for the discord between their parents. Autonomy requires us to develop the desire and skills to be independent and self-sufficient, to be able to depend more and more on ourselves as we grow.

When we are so tuned in to the external environment and the people in that environment that we try to control what happens, we disconnect from our own needs. Thus we risk that our needs will remain unmet, and we will feel a deep frustration. This is a pattern that Lakesha could carry forward if her grandparents do not interrupt that pattern by replacing it with their unconditional love and care.

The major challenge for parenting grandparents with grandchildren in this stage of development is to help your grandkids manage separation so that they can be more independent, which will help them establish good, personal boundaries, and also allow them to begin to separate fantasy from reality. Trauma or significant loss during this stage may lead to exaggerated sensitivities and fears of rejection, whereby these children feel insignificant, rather than self-assured. Your grandchildren's high need for your approval during this stage may be a sign that they are feeling powerless inside.

Discipline during this phase should be firm and consistent, but loving and understanding. One way to do this is to separate your grandchildren from their behavior. For example, "I want you to understand I love you very much, but I am giving you a timeout because it is not okay to hit your sister." Praise goes a long way for the four-, five-, and six-year-old. Limits, along with an explanation of the consequences if rules are broken, should be clear. Time-outs should be of a reasonable length of time. As a rule of thumb, a time-out should be equal in minutes to children's individual ages. So, if your granddaughter is four years old, a time-out of four minutes is reasonable; likewise, six minutes for your six-year-old grandson, and so on.

Remember, this stage is for playing! Limit the time spent in front of the television and computer, and encourage your grandchildren to play. Whether your grandchildren play alone or with other children, play is an important activity for the development of the imagination and early social skills. Along with play, this is also the "praise" stage; genuine praise goes a long way with children during this phase.

Stage 4: Learning Industry versus Inferiority

According to Erikson, the fourth developmental stage occurs during what he terms the *school age*, approximately from the ages of six to eleven. During this stage, your grandchildren learn to master the more formal skills of life: (1) relating with peers and friends, according to rules; (2) progressing from free play to play that may be structured by rules, and also that may demand teamwork of some kind, such as soccer or baseball; and (3) mastering schoolwork. Homework is a necessity, and the need for self-discipline increases yearly. The degree to which your grandchildren are able to achieve the goals of this stage will depend on how well they mastered becoming autonomous and self-reliant during the previous developmental stages.

If your grandchildren have successfully moved through the earlier developmental stages, they should be trusting, autonomous, and full of initiative, and, as a result, being industrious and conscientious will not be difficult. During this stage, your grandchildren begin to discover and express their true self. They also learn to manage rules and authority, and they begin to experience a sense of competence and self-confidence.

However, mistrusting children will doubt the future. Children filled with shame and guilt experience feelings of defeat and inferiority, and/ or a sense of helplessness. With either too much competence or a false sense of confidence, children become adults too soon, losing their connection to childhood.

Children who experience trauma during this stage often feel excluded socially. They may fear other children who they perceive to be strong or dominant, because traumatized children consider themselves inferior. Some children may experience confusion around identity, especially as they approach eleven and twelve years of age.

Traumatic experiences during this developmental stage may signal a poor sense of self, and some children may seem as if they are not fully present. They may become less spontaneous and less confident, and more cautious and repressed. These children's need for approval is also high because of the internal instability that they experience.

This developmental stage focuses on concrete knowing and learning skills, and also on healthy cooperation. The main purpose of this stage is *learning skills,* which includes developing the ability to learn from mistakes, learning the consequences of breaking rules, as well as competing with and testing one's abilities as compared with the abilities of others.

If children are unable to manage this fourth stage of development, the symptoms of failure will manifest, including the belief that they must be perfect, along with the insistence that their own point of view must prevail. The opposite can also occur, wherein these children easily give in to peers and are too easily influenced by them. Inflexible values, represented as excessive stubbornness or a tendency toward impulsivity, are other signs of inferiority. Such children are prone to joining gangs or to being loners; either way, they challenge rules and authority, and usually are seen as rebellious.

> *Delbert, an eleven-year-old Navajo child, has been raised by his grandmother, Beatrice ever since his birth (his mother, Beatrice's daughter was a teen when he was born). Delbert and Beatrice live on the Navajo reservation in the Southwest US. Beatrice describes Delbert as reclusive, isolated, and detached. When I talked with Delbert, he barely spoke. He did share enough, however, for me to realize that he had a cognitive challenge marked by poor concentration and focus. Beatrice also described him as rebellious; Delbert continually rejects a lot of the rules for youngsters his age in the Navajo community.*
>
> *While Delbert is not a gang member at this time, he is at risk of becoming one. He does tend to identify with other peers who feel alienated from their community, if not society. He expresses resistance to both tribal rules and his grandmother's rules. Delbert's attitude reflects a disinterest in life, along with pessimism and aloofness.*

Behind Delbert's belligerent attitude lies a preadolescent filled with mistrust and shame. Given to his grandmother at birth, and later confused by his mother's unpredictable comings and goings, Delbert has come to believe that he does not deserve love and affection. He does not believe he is worthy of approval or recognition because he does not believe that he does anything well. He struggles in school as a result of his difficulty concentrating and his inability to focus. His poor self-esteem and feelings of inferiority cause him to avoid those peers who appear confident and successful. More and more, Delbert has begun to hang out with those who share a mistrust of the world.

Delbert might be helped with his school studies by an after-school program where he could receive some one-on-one support. In addition, the adults in his life, including his grandmother, need to offer Delbert genuine recognition and approval for the things that he does well. Again, giving Delbert the reassurance that he is loved, while simultaneously creating an environment that is predictable, will assist him in successfully managing his daily routines.

Finally, children whose parents are unpredictable and inconsistent in their contact with them often experience inner anxiety and frustration. This anxiety and frustration, while understandable, can frequently evidence as poor concentration, an inability to problem-solve, or even to sit still. As a parenting grandparent, you may need to seek counseling for your grandchildren so they can begin to verbalize their inner frustrations; and also, you may need to set some strict boundaries for visitation or phone calls by their parent(s). In some cases, grandparents have had to disallow any kind of interaction between their grandchildren and their biological parent(s) because the cost to the children's mental and emotional well-being was too high.

Summary

Children who successfully manage these first four stages of development have learned to trust, and so they demonstrate autonomy, initiative, and industry. These children are confident and competent, and they trust both their own internal world and the external world.

Children who have been frustrated and challenged by abandonment, trauma, rejection, and/or loss throughout these first four developmental stages are likely to be mistrustful, which breeds feelings of shame, guilt, and inferiority. These feelings generally are reflected in negative self-messaging. Children and teens begin to believe they are not good enough, not lovable, or that there must be something wrong with them.

Because these first four developmental stages involve a wide age range, the next section addresses suggestions for dealing with grandchildren between the ages of six and ten, and then with grandchildren between the ages of ten and twelve.

Six- to Ten-Year-Old Children

Tell your grandchildren every day how much you love them! At this age, children need to feel valued within the family and among friends. Words of affection go a long way—as do words of encouragement when the child struggles with homework or with any task. Be sure your words are heartfelt, as children sense the feelings behind our words.

At this age, your grandchildren will appreciate any personal space you can provide at home, even if that space is limited. Protect this personal space from intrusive siblings as much as possible. In fact, this may be a good space for you and your grandchildren to talk about school, friends, and feelings, and also for you to answer their questions.

One of the most important skills that children of this age can develop is an ability to deal constructively with conflict and anger in the family, at school, and in the neighborhood. As a parenting grandparent, you may want to make time weekly for a family meeting to discuss family matters.

Two techniques that can work very well in family meetings are:

1. Use a talking stick (it can be anything—a twig, a stone, or a small rock), and pass it around the family circle. Only the person with the talking stick can speak; everybody else listens. This ensures that younger children will have the same air time as older siblings, and also that less-talkative

kids have the same opportunity to speak as the "talkers" do.

2. Close each family meeting by having each family member say: "I need more of _____." "I need less of _____." "I need the same of _____." No one comments; everyone just listens and tries to behave in a way that meets each family member's identified need during the time that follows the meeting.

As an example, let's say we are closing a family meeting. In the beginning of this practice, you may begin by stating: "I need to see more respect for each other's quiet time. I need to hear less squabbling in the morning when everyone is getting ready for school, and I need to continue to receive the same amount of hugs and kisses that each of you has been giving me." Your grandchild might say: "I need you to be more patient with me. I need less nagging about doing my homework. I need the same amount of complements and recognition you have been giving me."

As your family gets used to this practice, you can have your grandchildren take turns starting the "I need" comments. Children take this practice quite seriously when adults role model good listening skills, and good support, by honoring what everyone has said. I remember a seven-year-old who closed a family meeting by saying: "I need everyone who plays with my toys to put them away nicely when they're finished playing with them. I need less lectures about doing my homework from Grandma, and I don't know what I need the same of!"

Children will be age-appropriate when doing this activity, as long as they know their grandparents will make sure that everyone follows the rules of listening and responding. This format is a great way to find out what is on your grandchildren's minds, what may be bothering them, and what is really working for them. Remember that no one is allowed to comment on what anyone else says—whether they agree or disagree. This shows respect for each family member's thoughts, concerns, desires, etc.

Finally, grandparents need to establish fair rules with respect to chores, TV watching, video games, computer use, outside activities, homework, bedtime, etc. The number of rules should be kept to a minimum, so that your grandchildren know what is really important in your family. Children of this age respond well to charts, a calendar that shows everyone's schedule, and stars or stickers as recognition of achievement next to their names. Making a chart for their chores, appointments, and homework schedules offers one way of showing grandchildren how to organize themselves and develop good routines, which, in turn, will help them feel independent and in charge of themselves.

The role of peers in the life of six- to ten-year-olds increases as they grow, so be sure to know who their friends are; have them over as much as possible so that you can get to know them. Knowing your grandchildren's friends is very important.

Finally, as bedtimes approach, grandparents should encourage reading or storytelling together. Your example will help reinforce that both activities give pleasure. And, as fatigue can be a factor as we age, when you get really tired, you can always watch some TV together.

Ten- to Twelve-Year-Old Children

Dramatic physical changes are the hallmark of early adolescence. Therefore, preadolescents (or as they are sometimes called, "tweens") will need reassurance that their growth and development are normal. Also, it's good to let them know that everyone's body changes uniquely, so some of their peers will grow taller and develop faster, while others will have slower physiological changes. Re-assure them that whatever way and speed their own body changes occur is perfect for them. As a rule, girls develop and change earlier than most boys do, but again, for many preadolescents, physical and emotional changes seem to appear earlier than when we grandparents were their age—or when their parents were their age.

At this age, your grandchildren may suddenly become preoccupied with their appearance and/or attractiveness. Clothes, makeup, hairstyles, diet, even the expressions they use to communicate with each other suddenly take center stage.

> *When one of my granddaughters turned eleven, she began to refer to everyone as "dude." I noticed that gender did not seem to matter as she referred to both her male and female friends as "dudes." One day, she even referred to me as "dude," but I was not able to respond to that very well. The word rolled off her tongue without the slightest discernment, which is pretty typical of preteens and teens, and I told her in a neutral tone that I didn't like being called "dude." We had a good laugh and five years later, I remain Grandma to her—and sometimes "G-dog," when I have done something she really considers "beastin' or "sick." which, in our day, we called "cool!"*

Most twelve-year-olds focus on social life, friends, and school. One day you are their confidantes, and the next day you have been dropped like an anchor for a best friend who has suddenly become the "wise counsel." These friendships, however, may change abruptly, causing hurt feelings and confusion. Needless to say, a lot of personal angst will be brought into your home when this happens. What once seemed a calm, fun-loving environment can, overnight, become one of tension, tears, and turmoil. One of my daughters, who is the mother of three teen girls, calls this the "Thirteen Syndrome."

Despite all the hormones produced by your preteens' bodies, they need to respect the rights and needs of everyone in the family. You may need to be a bit more patient and cut them some slack as they adjust to their new bodies; but again, the values you've taught them remain the foundation for acceptable behaviors. Part of learning respect is following family rules, such as those for curfews, computer use, television, telephone/texting time, dinnertime, bedtime, and household chores.

School activities are important in the life of a twelve-year-old. Social activities often center on sports events and school dances. Just because your grandchild is becoming more social does not mean you need to give up your family meetings or time together. Flexible schedules may begin to rule the day and the week; however, each week should have a time when everyone is together. I used to make this time during Sunday dinner. All my daughters knew that they had to be present for dinner, no matter where they had gone for the day. Bringing a friend over for Sunday dinner was okay. It made for a more festive time together, but, no matter what, my daughters had to be home for Sunday dinner.

As a grandparent, one of your most important responsibilities is to serve as a positive ethical and behavioral role model. The younger your grandchildren are when you begin setting expectations for them as members of your family, the more likely they will be to comply with family norms as they enter adolescence.

Developmental stages 1 through 4 have to do with your grandchildren figuring out the world. Stages 5 through 7, which part II of this chapter will address, are about your grandchildren figuring themselves out; or, more specifically, their tasks in these next three stages are to answer the question, "Who am I?"

Gentle Reminders

1. A developmental stage is an expected and sequential order by which we develop life skills through the accomplishment of developmental tasks. It begins at infancy (stage 1) and continues through old age (stage 8).

2. In order to gain a deeper understanding of the developmental stages, you can visit some of the websites listed below. This information will be both instructive and helpful to you in setting appropriate expectations and boundaries for your grandchildren as they move through each developmental stage:

* psychology.about.com/library/bl_psychosocial_summary.htm

* www.learningplaceonline.com/stages/organize/Erikson.htm

* www.childdevelopmentinfo.com › child development

3. During the period between infancy and the preteen years, babies, toddlers, and children need to build a sense of trust with their primary caregivers. This provides the underpinnings for the trust that they need in order to grow, and also to feel safe and secure in the world. Toddlers begin to become more independent and self-reliant as a result of this foundation of trust. This, in turn, leads to a growing sense of autonomy as they begin to explore and discover the world around them.

As children enter school, their developmental challenge is to develop a sense of initiative, learning to take risks and try new things. They begin to learn about themselves and the world around them. This marks the beginning of the long road to learning and building new skills.

With a foundation built on trust, autonomy, and initiative, the latency-aged child begins to take on the new challenges of working in a group or on a team. With confidence, they become more industrious and conscientious about their work and play. Cooperation, accountability, and responsibility become the basic traits through which they negotiate their world.

Anything that interrupts their ability to master these developmental skills—such as trauma, illness, or loss—can delay a child's mastery of these developmental stages. Awareness of their needs, family and professional support, patience, and unconditional love all will help them meet their developmental challenges successfully, even if it comes at a later period.

4. No matter which developmental stage your grandchildren are in, the need for love, safety, and security will always be a top priority. The need for consistency and predictability is also vital.

PART II: WHO AM I?

Erikson's next four developmental stages focus on each individual's trying to figure out who he or she is as a person. These stages range from adolescence to the elder years. (We will discuss stage 8, which focuses on elder developmental issues, in chapter 5.)

Our ability to emerge from childhood with an individualized identity depends on whether our early life supported the development of the capacity to trust life—that is, to be an autonomous individual who is sufficiently industrious to be capable of defining personal goals and demonstrating the initiative to achieve them.

Some children will emerge quite ready to embrace life; however, others, who have an innate mistrust of life that is complicated by a sense of shame, guilt, or inferiority, will create barriers to their own growth and progress. The following case study, involving Hanna and Jack, demonstrates the remarkable impact that parenting grandparents can have on their grandchildren, especially on their ability to master the tasks of each developmental life stage.

> *Brandon and Billy came to live with their grandmother, Hanna, when they were three and one year-old, respectively. Both of their parents were addicted to drugs and neglecting the boys. They have been in and out of jail over the last seven years and have given custody of both boys, now thirteen and eleven years-old, to Hanna.*
>
> *Hanna raised six children of her own, all of whom, with the exception of her son, Jon (Brandon and Billy's dad), are doing fine, employed, and raising Hanna's eighteen other grandchildren. Hanna, a seventy-*

five-year-old widow, remarried; her second husband, Jack is seventy-three years old.

Hanna began her story by telling me how the boys' mother, Amy, would make false promises that enraged Brandon and Billy. Before her imprisonment, Amy would tell Hanna that she planned to visit the boys, but she rarely showed up; often, if she did visit, she arrived high on drugs, or drunk. Amy would promise to call the boys, but, for the most part, she never did. Hanna said that, after a while of this, Brandon would say, "The 'no-show' will never come, and she won't call either, and I don't even want to see her anymore." When he did see Amy, Brandon would tell her, "You're a mom. You are not supposed to lie."

The disappointment children feel begins like a scratch on the skin. As time passes, and that disappointment feels more like rejection, that scratch becomes a serious wound. It is important to remember that, unlike a flesh wound that we can see, this wound is psychological and emotional, and so it is not necessarily visible. However, it is no less painful, and it is equally essential to address so that it can properly heal.

Brandon, at age seven, has already learned to mistrust his biological mother. Consequently, both Brandon and Billy are at high risk for mistrusting life in general. Their relationship with their grandparents is what will provide the opportunity for a corrective experience, whereby these boys can encounter life as caring, predictable, and consistent. Otherwise, Brandon and Billy may well be struggling to manage the first developmental stage, "trust versus mistrust," for a very long time.

With their early years built on the wobbly foundation of mistrust—including the constant disappointment caused by their biological mother's neglect in her duties as their primary caregiver—it will be hard for Brandon and Billy to experience autonomy or self-sufficiency. Traversing the developmental stages of life is considerably more difficult when the first step of the ladder is fragile and weak. Their grandparents' love and guidance are the only things that might make it possible for both boys to succeed developmentally.

Again, we see why the work of parenting grandparents is so very sacred and noble. Brandon and Billy have received a decent chance at a successful life only because of Hanna and Jack. Theirs will not be an easy journey, but the sacrifice parenting grandparents often make for their grandchildren is selfless and meaningful. It is the difference between having a life and being a victim of life, of being loved or not being loved, of feeling self-confident or feeling inferior. Giving our grandchildren the opportunity to greet life with optimism and trust is a gift of the heart, and it is the finest gift children can receive from their grandparents. (We'll continue Hanna and Jack's story in chapter 5, when reviewing the tasks associated with their own final phase of life [stage 8].)

Now let's take a quick look at our brain chemistry, and how it impacts our ability to traverse the challenges of growing up and successfully handling the tasks of each stage of development. We will also examine how trauma, in particular, negatively affects our brain chemistry.

In the United States, social researchers say that, based upon brain chemistry, adolescence extends through age twenty-five. Those who study both Emotional Intelligence and Social Intelligence now are finding the limbic system of the brain, where emotions are processed, to be slower than originally thought. In order to move beyond this part of the brain to the prefrontal lobe, which is where we organize information, process it logically and rationally, solve problems, and make decisions, we must create neural connections.[14]

These connections are a result of neural pathways, which are created by repetitive patterns or behaviors often referred to as *habits*. Adolescents and young adults who emerge from nurturing and growth-oriented family environments create neural pathways that support communication and connection between the limbic system of the brain and the prefrontal cortex. Behavioral processes reflect both the ability to process emotions and thoughts in a productive, balanced way, especially as we grow from adolescence to young adulthood.[15]

Those who experienced environments lacking in nurturance and love have neural pathways that produce a hypervigilance, defending against anything that might threaten the individual's physical, mental, emotional, or social safety and security. The good news, however, is that, at any age, the brain is capable of creating new neural pathways through cultivating positive, new habits.

This point is important for parenting grandparents to know and understand. It underscores the opportunity you have to influence your grandchildren in positive, loving, and nurturing ways. The key is consistency and repetition of positive behaviors and messages, which, in the long run, will help your grandchildren become more trusting, confident, and successful at achieving the goals of their individual developmental stages.

This recent research into the realms of Emotional and Social Intelligence expands our understanding of the developmental challenges that people face as they grow into adulthood. It also provides a sense of hope and optimism that our grandchildren can master the challenges of childhood and adolescence, despite the setbacks they may have experienced related to their biological parents.

Stage 5: Learning Identity versus Identity Diffusion

During this fifth stage, from about age thirteen to the early twenties, every adolescent learns how to satisfactorily answer the question, "Who am I?" But even the most-well-adjusted adolescents experience some role diffusion, where the sense of self is unsteady and prone to feeling threatened. During this period, most boys and girls experiment with minor delinquency; also, here is the stage during which rebellion flourishes, and self-doubt can overwhelm.

Teens and young adults attempt to develop their identities and ideas about strengths, weaknesses, occupations, sexual orientation, and gender roles. Teens try on different identities, frequently experience identity crises, and use their friends to reflect and support them. If they successfully move through this phase, they develop fidelity or reliability, which is the ability to sustain loyalties and become friends with very different people.

During successful early adolescence, the goal is for young people to acquire self-certainty, as opposed to self-consciousness and self-doubt. The challenge for teens is to experiment with different constructive roles, rather than adopting negative identities, such as "delinquent" or "deviant."

In later adolescence, clear sexual identity–manhood or womanhood—is established. Adolescents also seek leadership—role models to inspire them—and they gradually develop a set of ideals that are either congruent with society or antagonistic to societal norms.

During this developmental stage, teens need to develop a sense of self and personal identity. Success leads to an ability to stay true to one's self, while failure leads to role confusion and a vulnerable sense of self.

Traumas during this stage often leave many adolescents feeling vulnerable and confused, many may also develop a fear of intimacy because they feel so fragile. Some teens may express frustration that they have no clear purpose and find no meaning in life. Internally, they may feel a sense of emptiness. This sense contributes to their drift toward others who also internally feel like misfits, potentially leading to membership in gangs, the use of alcohol and other drugs, and behaviors that further alienate teens from their families and society at large.

This next story will reveal some of the very serious types of trauma that can occur to children who have endured both abandonment and abuse. It will also reveal the impact that trauma has on teens moving through this stage of development.

Eleven years ago, Rachel, now seventy-six years old, moved to Indiana to retire to a place where she had long desired to live. One month after moving, Rachel received a call from Child Protective Services of Chicago asking her to come and get her six-year-old grandson, Tommy, whose parents were abusing him, both physically and emotionally. Rachel went to Chicago to get Tommy, taking him to live with her in Indiana.

With some guilt in her voice, Rachel said, "Every day, for a long time, I thought about how I was supposed to retire, take life easy, and enjoy my old age. Instead, I became a mother again: Tommy has lived with me for eleven years." Over time, Rachel received calls from the Chicago court to come and get Tommy's siblings, Sam and Lila, also.

As she became a parenting grandmother, Rachel learned about a group of grandparents headquartered in South Bend, Indiana. They call themselves G.A.P. (Grandparents As Parents). During the interview process, I met several G.A.P. members, along with the group's president, and found them to be passionate, strong, and devoted not only to their grandchildren and to one another within the group, but also to helping and supporting other parenting grandparents.

Rachel said that the toughest part of her role was dealing with the confusing and chaotic relationship Tommy has with his biological mother. She described Tommy, more so than his siblings, as having deep rage and fear.

Rachel began to cry as she told me that Tommy was diagnosed with Post-Traumatic Stress Disorder (PTSD) as a result of the abuse and abandonment by his parents. PTSD is an anxiety disorder that can develop after exposure to a terrifying event or ordeal in which grave physical harm occurred or in which the person was threatened.[16]

By the time Tommy was six years old, he had heard many threatening remarks and had seen aggressive behaviors by his father toward both his mother and himself. He lived in constant fear and anxiety. Tommy was even afraid for his grandmother's life, as his parents had entered Rachel's house illegally several times, causing her to change her locks frequently.

At age fourteen, Tommy still struggled with his mother's rejection. He would tell Rachel, "You are raising me, Grandma. You are my mom. But I love Sara, too; she is also my mom."

Tommy tried to commit suicide when he was ten, feeling deep despair that neither of his biological parents wanted him; but, in particular, it was Sara's rejection that caused Tommy the most pain. This case shows extreme consequences of abuse and abandonment. Tommy no longer wanted to be in this world, feeling both unsafe with and rejected by his biological parents. Rejection, together with physical and emotional abuse, led Tommy to conclude that he was not lovable—and he was powerless to do anything about the situation. Even his grandmother's love was not enough to fill the emptiness that he experienced. Tommy turned his angst and rage against himself, and he attempted to end his own life.

Rachel told me that Tommy has since been diagnosed with Bipolar Disorder, and he is on medication and in treatment. He remains with his grandmother, and she describes him as fairly uncommunicative. He will talk with his counselor, whom he sees weekly, and with his younger siblings on occasion.

When I asked Rachel how she deals with such an extreme situation, she tearfully told me that she believes Tommy will come around when he's ready. She said the counselor told her he has to build up his trust and confidence in his significant relationships, and then he will be able to learn who he can relate to and who won't betray him.

Developmentally, as a baby and as a toddler, Tommy learned that he could not trust his world to keep him safe and secure. His boundaries had been shattered by physical and emotional abuse, and, because of his age, he was dependent on biological parents who rejected and abused him. He could not bond with parents, who were perpetrators instead of protectors, and this left him with major attachment issues.

For his own safety, Tommy had to be taken from his biological parents, and then he had to learn to trust his grandmother and his new environment. This likely would have happened if not for the threats made by his parents toward his grandmother. In his mind, Tommy may have fearfully thought, "If the one person who loves me and keeps me safe is threatened, then what happens to me?" This thought, together with the chaos in the relationship with his biological mother who betrayed many promises that she made to Tommy, contributed to his withdrawal and isolation. Over and over again, Tommy learned he could not trust the people who brought him into the world, and his grandmother's attempts to keep him safe and secure were sabotaged by his biological parents' threats and broken promises. Eventually, Rachel, who obtained guardianship for all three of her grandchildren, had to get a court order to keep Tommy's parents away.

Rachel told me that Tommy is doing much better now, as a result of both his treatment for Bipolar Disorder and the fact that he has no contact with either of his biological parents. Even though he is now seventeen years old, developmentally, he still struggles with accomplishing the tasks of the first developmental stage: trust versus mistrust.

His chronological age suggests that he should be working on developing an identity and a sense of self. But Tommy's past has him struggling with identity diffusion, meaning that his sense of self is unsteady and easily threatened. It may take Tommy many more years to accomplish what his peers are now able to achieve. Because of the deep love of his grandmother, Tommy's chances of developing and succeeding in life are significantly better than they were when he was with his biological parents or potentially facing foster care.

Rachel's sacrifices, like those of many parenting grandparents, cannot be minimized. While Rachel and Tommy's story is severe and extreme, it is not unusual. Many grandparents interviewed had to deal with Child Protective Services, as well as other legal and family-service agencies, in order to protect their grandchildren from their biological parents. Again, we see why the work of grandparents who raise their grandchildren is so sacred and so noble.

The Parent and Child Guidance Center of Pittsburgh, Pennsylvania, recommends some reminders for parenting grandparents of teens, including:

- Times are different now than when we were teens. Adolescents have many more obstacles to overcome than we did when we were going through the same physical and emotional changes. In addition, many new life issues exist now, which people of all ages must learn to handle.

- The teen years can be an extremely difficult time. Grandparents must learn to cope with their adolescents, while simultaneously trying to keep the channels of communication open. Love with no strings attached. You will find yourself growing in wisdom as you struggle with the issues that teens force us to confront.

Here are some basic survival strategies for parenting grandparents of adolescents:

1. *Choose your battles carefully.* Settle for something less than perfection on issues that don't really matter. Remain calm, and don't match the level of emotional intensity that your teens display.

2. *Intense emotions pass.* Save the important part of a conversation with your teens for when emotions are calmer for both of you.

3. *Be available to adolescents without directing or controlling them.* The time when they will want you is often at the teens' choosing, not yours. Be there when they need you.

4. *Establish networks with the parents of your teens' friends.* Make it a point to get to know them, even if they are new to you—and a lot younger than you are.

5. *Make sure you and your teens know what the priorities are in your home*—keeping curfews, staying free of drugs and alcohol, eating dinner together, play and recreational time, doing chores and homework, having difficult conversations instead of avoiding them, maintaining respect for self and family, etc.

6. *Let teens know they can always call you when in trouble*—without fear of recrimination.

And some final words of wisdom:

•   Do not dismiss feelings of sadness and depression as normal moodiness for teens. Situational losses—including the death of a pet, problems with girlfriends or boyfriends, school failure, and/or parental disappointment or absence—all can lead to depression and even suicide. If you are concerned that your teen(s) may be suffering from depression, consult a doctor or counselor for advice.

•   Remember that peer acceptance is extremely important to adolescents. The group sets standards for behavior, and rejection can be devastating. Listen to your grandchildren when situations occur that separate them from the group. Talk about it together, knowing you don't necessarily have to give advice. Furthermore, although it can be difficult, learn to adjust to the variations in hair and clothing. Try your best to be flexible.

- To be of most benefit to growing adolescents, grandparents need to remain constant and consistent figures; they should be available as sounding boards for teens' ideas, but without dominating or overtaking the emerging, independent identity of these adolescents.

Stage 6: Learning Intimacy versus Isolation

Young adults—ranging in age from the mid-twenties to the mid-thirties—who have successfully moved through the first five developmental stages are now ready and able to experience true intimacy for the first time. True intimacy makes possible both genuine, enduring friendships and good, stable marriages. Intimacy is the ability to be close, loving, and self-revealing in romances and friendships. In part, intimacy is based upon identity development, insofar as people need to know themselves in order to be able share themselves with another. The virtue gained as a result of true intimacy is love.

Success during this stage leads to strong relationships, while failure results in loneliness and feelings of isolation. In addition, failure to develop intimacy can lead to promiscuity (getting too close too quickly and then not being able to sustain the relationship) or exclusion (rejecting relationships and avoiding people who have solid relationships). Children and adolescents who have not resolved their earlier developmental tasks may express a sense of unworthiness and alienation during this stage of young adulthood.

The adult children of many parenting grandparents describe themselves as feeling isolated and alienated from their families, communities, and society. Many of them have criminal records or are in jail; some are challenged by addictions that prevent them from successful employment; still others are in gangs or groups that engage in deviant behaviors.

Because of these and other reasons, the grandparents have become parents to their grandchildren.

Let's take another look at Ann's family (this is the parenting grandparent whose story we began to explore in the introduction).

Susan is a forty-year-old mom. Her son, James, is fourteen, and her daughter, Kayli, is four; the children have different fathers. Susan's twin brother, Sam, is married, has a college degree, and is employed full-time.

For the first fourteen years of their lives, the twins' mother, Ann, raised both children, with the help of her own parents. Because of his deviant behaviors, Ann had divorced her husband—her children's biological father—when the twins were a year old. Ann remarried when the twins were fifteen, and her second husband, John, later adopted them.

Growing up, Susan was a rambunctious, happy-go-lucky child who did not seem affected by the absence of her biological father. Ann noticed that her daughter's short attention span and inability to focus contributed to some school challenges, but, overall, she felt that Susan had adjusted as well as possible to the challenges of having a single, working mom. Plus, Ann's own parents offered her daily support in helping to raise the twins, which allowed Ann to work full-time outside the home.

As Susan entered junior high school, she began to display some self-doubt related to her competence at school and in social situations. She was also becoming impulsive and secretive. This worsened as she entered high school, and she began to complain about feeling inferior to her female classmates and cousins. Susan enrolled in the high school's vocational program that would prepare her for a career in hairstyling, but she began skipping school. Although she graduated from high school, Susan did not receive her vocational certificate because she lacked the number of hours that the program required.

After high school, Susan began hanging around with people who had alienated themselves from their families and communities, used drugs, and had a cynical view of life in general. Despite Ann's and her parents' (Susan's grandparents) best efforts, Susan alienated herself from her family, and her life began to spiral downward.

When interviewed, Susan described herself as "never having fit in." During high school, she began gaining weight, which increased her feelings of isolation and inferiority. Skipping school became her coping mechanism for the classes that overwhelmed her or that she believed she could not master. Over time, Susan developed a negative identity, which manifested in acting-out behaviors.

Instead of staying true to herself, which results from a sense of personal identity developed during the teen years, Susan began to experience role confusion, a weak sense of self, and feelings of inferiority. Instead of self-confidence, Susan felt self-doubt, which reinforced itself as she had continual trouble securing and keeping employment. She felt that she just never could measure up.

As Susan's sense of inferiority intensified over time, it led to identity diffusion during her teen years; from our definition, we know that this manifests as an unstable and easily threatened sense of self.

By the time Susan was in her twenties, it was evident that she was unable to experience intimacy in her relationships. Once again, intimacy requires the ability to be close, loving, and vulnerable with friends and romantic partners. Instead, Susan experienced loneliness and isolation. Without a clear sense of self, it is impossible to know yourself or share yourself in a mature way. All of Susan's friendships were with other people who struggled with their identities, acted out in rebellious ways, and engaged in unhealthy behaviors.

Susan was unable to manage the developmental challenge of intimacy versus isolation because she was unsuccessful in resolving earlier developmental stages. The cumulative effect created a young woman with an ever-increasing sense of unworthiness, which manifested as alienation during her young-adult stage.

By her late twenties, Susan was drug- and alcohol-dependent, promiscuous, and unable to hold a job for more than six months. She had two abortions before giving birth to her son, James. Susan lived with James's father, but they did not marry. The relationship was abusive, and the home environment was unsafe for both Susan and James.

After James's father's arrest and incarceration for criminal behavior, Susan was left alone to take care of James. At this point, Ann became involved in supporting both Susan and James. She provided James with his basic needs, kept him at her home on weekends when she was not at work, and offered him a stable, secure home environment. She also provided occasional financial support to Susan to help pay the rent on her apartment. Over time, the occasional financial support became more frequent; this increased frequency began to irritate both Ann and Susan.

By the time she was in her thirties, Susan was unable to care for herself or her son without Ann's support. She continued hanging out with people who were a negative influence, and, in a sense, she became a lost soul. With her partner still in prison, Susan dated other deviant men, and continued to entangle herself in short-lived, troublesome relationships.

This story exemplifies how early abandonment—in this case, by Susan's biological father—contributed to a growing sense of unworthiness during her development. (We will continue this story in the next section, which covers stage 7.) Over and over again, Susan would ask, "How could your own parent not want anything to do with you? I just don't understand that. He is out there somewhere, but he just doesn't want anything to do with me."

Susan's question implies her own unspoken conclusion about herself: "There must be something wrong with me. I must not be good enough." During Susan's teen years, as school became more of a challenge and the adolescent social life became more competitive, thoughts of self-doubt as to who she was as a person filled Susan's psyche, reinforcing her conclusion that something was "wrong" with her and she was "not good enough."

Also implied in Susan's repeated question is the sense of betrayal that she continues to feel in regard to her biological father. She confirmed this during her interview: "He helped create me, and then he disappeared. How could he walk away from his own flesh and blood?" That betrayal is the deep wound of abandonment. Throughout children's and teens' development, that wound will fester if life's circumstances verify that they are "not good enough." This is exactly what happened to Susan: She was unable to keep up in school, felt left out of peer groups, compared herself to her female classmates and cousins, and concluded that she was just not good enough. Over and over again, Susan felt that life had been cruel and unfair to her, and she could not get past that. By the time she reached young adulthood, her life was in turmoil.

The hole that abandonment creates in a person's heart is hard to fill—even for adults, let alone children and teens. However, it is not impossible to fill that hole, heal, and live a meaningful and successful life. Parenting grandparents have the opportunity to help their grandchildren achieve this healing. It is so very important to seek guidance, support, and counseling if your grandchildren show signs of self-loathing, or overly self-critical, or seem emotionally and/or psychologically stuck in wrong and harsh conclusions about themselves. This is true no matter what age they are or what developmental stage they are in.

Stage 7: Learning Generativity versus Stagnation

Our current social norms and the Baby Boomer generation have extended this developmental stage considerably. Think of this stage as having two phases: thirty to fifty years of age, and fifty to seventy years of age.

This developmental stage of adulthood demands *generativity,* or the ability to produce, both in the sense of successful relationships and parenthood, and also in the sense of working productively and creatively. People who have a strong sense of creativity, success, and goal accomplishment will develop generativity; as such, they develop concern for the "next generation," even if they do not become parents. This stage develops the virtue of caring, and it represents your connection to the future.

Adults who do not feel this innate caring may become self-absorbed, feel little connection to others, and generally offer little to society. Erikson calls this *stagnation.* Excessive stagnation can lead to a failure to experience any sense of meaning or purpose in life, which we sometimes refer to as a "midlife crisis." At the same time, excessive generativity can lead to individuals having little or no time for themselves because they are so busy caring for the younger generation.

This last statement has significance for parenting grandparents: It is a reminder to be sure to take good care of yourself, as well as your grandchildren. Parenting grandparents, as much as possible, need to maintain their close friendships, enjoy walks in nature, participate in social activities, and actively engage in anything else that gives meaning and purpose to their lives.

To further illustrate this developmental stage, let's continue Susan and Ann's story.

> *At age thirty-six, Susan became pregnant again, by another man who would not be available to help her raise the child. At this point, Susan was despondent, and her health began to fail after the birth of her daughter, Kayli. Caring for Kayli was a far bigger challenge than she had anticipated. Her life, despite being the mother of two children, seemed to revolve around a constant barrage of her own problems.*

Susan did not ever feel healthy or well, which was the result of complications related to her pregnancy and to obesity. In addition, she was alone, unemployed, and overwhelmed by having to care for her ten-year-old son, James, and her infant daughter, Kayli. James was having trouble with his schoolwork, and his home life was chaotic.

At about the age eleven, James went to live with his grandmother, Ann. Enrolled in a new school, and receiving constant, unconditional love and nurturing that all children require, James felt secure and safe for the first time. His grades gradually improved; today, at thirteen, James is an honor-roll student.

Susan, now forty, continues to struggle with the same issues that she battled during her twenties. She is jobless and has not received the treatment interventions that she so desperately needs; as a result, she continues to struggle with her physical health, her relationships, and her feelings of guilt, shame, and inferiority. Because of all her unresolved issues, Susan still struggles with the consequences of the poor decisions she has made in the past—more to the point, she continues to make poor decisions, many of which have negatively affected both her children's and her own well-being.

Despite every intention of wanting to do better, to be more independent, to feel better physically and emotionally, Susan has not been able to find the confidence and inner resources to "turn the corner." At times, Susan appears to exhibit self-absorption and self-entitlement—that is, her expectation that she is "entitled" to financial support from the state and from her mother, as well as state-provided health insurance and healthcare.

These traits are not unusual among adults who believe that life has not treated them fairly. Susan describes an inner rage toward her biological father, who has been absent from her life since she was a year old. The understandable anger that she felt as a result of this abandonment, but that she did not express during her childhood, turned to rage when

Susan was in her teens; at some point during her twenties, Susan turned that rage against herself.

At this point in her life, Susan displays what Erikson referred to as *stagnation,* the failure to develop an innate sense of caring for the generations to come, which presents as self-absorption—that is, feeling little connection to others, and, in general, taking from rather than giving to society. Chronologically, Susan is forty years old, but, developmentally, she has not managed to learn to trust herself or the outside world; she remains dependent instead of independent, and her feelings of inferiority continue to overwhelm her. Mentally and emotionally, Susan is stuck in an earlier developmental stage, and needs counseling to help her traverse the obstacles which prevent her healing and growth.

As a parenting grandparent, Ann has made every effort to help her daughter achieve the life success she desires. However, lacking the internal resources and refusing to seek the counseling that might have helped her successfully move through the developmental stages, Susan remains frustrated and overwhelmed by the challenges of everyday life.

As parenting grandparents, it is important to remember that these developmental stages build on each other. The stages are like a staircase: If the first step is missing, it is harder to get to the second step, and, even if we do, the absence of that first step weakens the foundation for all the other steps. When the first developmental stage of trust versus mistrust is weak—whether because of neglect, abuse, abandonment, or loss—it is hard, but not impossible, to navigate the other stages successfully.

As parenting grandparents, you have engaged in the sacred and noble work of providing your grandchildren with the foundation that they require in order to grow physically, mentally, emotionally, and socially, and thereby become successful adults. Despite the complexities of dealing with your adult children who cannot, for whatever reason, raise their own children, you still can provide for your grandchildren the safety and security that they need and deserve. As we do that for our grandchildren, we are gifting them with the foundation that will help them each achieve a fulfilling life.

Achieving fulfillment in life is a daunting task, and children and teens who have had strong role models are more likely to succeed than those who have not. Psychologist Abraham Maslow developed a model of motivation based on needs, organized from the most basic physiological requirements, through more complex emotional needs, and culminating in the need to develop one's innate potential. The model, often depicted as a pyramid, shows the more basic needs at the bottom and the more complex needs at the peak. Maslow's theory further states that we must satisfy our survival needs first; only then will we be motivated to fulfill our higher-level needs.

Maslow included five sets of goals, or basic needs, in his hierarchy.[17] These are the need for self-actualization, esteem needs, love and belongingness needs, safety needs, and physiological needs.

- **Self-Actualization Needs** – personal growth and fulfillment, creativity, etc. *(higher level needs))*

- **Esteem Needs** – achievement, status, responsibility, reputation, confidence, respect for and by others, etc.

- **Love and Belongingness Needs** – family, affection, relationships, intimacy, etc.

- **Safety Needs** – protection, security, order, stability, limits, etc

- **Physiological Needs** – basic life needs: clean air, water, food, shelter, sleep, sex, etc. *(basic needs))*

Beginning at the first or basic level, physiological needs, we provide our grandchildren with life's basic requirements. When those needs are met well, children feel safe, secure and are able to move *up* the growth pyramid to achieve a sense of being loved and belonging to a family. It is only then that we can achieve the higher and more complex level of needs. At this level, we acquire a sense of self-esteem and self-actualization. Remember, when basic needs are frustrated it is impossible to feel safe, secure and loved. It is impossible to grow and achieve our full potential.

Keep in mind that children are incredibly resilient, but they do need sustained nurturing and care, and unconditional love. Your grandchildren will demand a good deal of patience and understanding from you. Despite your best efforts to meet their needs, if you notice that any or all of your grandchildren appear to regress to behaviors of a younger age, act out behaviorally, display increased moodiness or temper tantrums, withdraw, or become very self-critical, seek professional guidance.

Many of your grandchildren have experienced deep-seated traumas, and the younger they are when they receive professional help, the more likely they will be able to heal from their psychological and emotional wounds. Also, the younger they are when they receive treatment intervention, the better chance they have of successfully mastering the developmental life stages.

The seven stages of development discussed up this point are plausible and insightful descriptions of how the human personality develops; however, at present, they are descriptions only. Helping our grandchildren through the various stages of life, and the positive learning that should accompany them, is a complex and difficult task, as all concerned grandparents know—not just parenting grandparents.

Despite the challenges you face as parenting grandparents, remember this: with your age comes the gift of wisdom. In other words, you are wise enough to know the importance of the greatest gift of all: unconditional love. Imagine what the world would be like if we each received love simply for being who we are, as we are! This is exactly the way that grandparents love grandchildren, and, as parenting grandparents, it is even more important to love your grandchildren unconditionally. This is the wisdom of the heart that you can teach—and give—every day.

Recently, I was texting with my oldest granddaughter, now eighteen and away at college. I wrote, "I love my VSG" (very special granddaughter). She texted me right back, "And I love my VSG" (very special grandma). So we both are VSGs, and it is not based on anything except a relationship of mutual unconditional love. Regardless of your grandchildren's struggles, let them know, each and every day, how very special they are to you and how much you love them. Love is the best antidote for any problem that gnaws at us, regardless of how old we are.

Gentle Reminders

1. Children's developmental ages can be very different from their chronological ages. Children who experience deep traumas, such as abandonment, abuse, and/or neglect may be psychologically, emotionally, and/or socially regressed, or "stuck," at an earlier developmental age. For example, if you see your eleven-year-old grandchild acting like a four-year-old on a consistent basis, consult your pediatrician for an evaluation.

2. Many websites offer information about the developmental stages children, adolescents, and adults move through as they grow, including:

   www.childdevelopmentinfo.com
   www.Education.com
   www.RevolutionHealth.com
   http://dormont-brookline.patch.com//listings/parent-child-guidance-center....Pittsburgh, PA

3. No one provides more unconditional love and understanding than a grandparent. Think of yourselves as "wisdom keepers"; you innately know what your grandchildren need and how to provide it.

5
THE ELDER LIFE STAGE

PART I: INTEGRITY VERSUS DESPAIR

This entire chapter will focus on Erikson's final developmental phase (stage 8): "integrity versus despair." This stage brings its own challenges, demands, and adjustments—to endings, losses, and, ultimately, death. But for parenting grandparents in this stage of life, the challenge is far more complex. Let's review stage 8, and then we'll look at how being a parenting grandparent complicates your ability to manage this final stage of life.

Stage 8: Integrity versus Despair

This is the final stage of life as we know it. As we approach the age of seventy, we begin to experience a sense of our own mortality. Whether it is in response to retirement, death (either of a spouse, siblings, and/or close friends), or our own inevitable physical and mental changes, this sense of mortality entails facing the end of life. We face the end of our life by accepting our successes, failures, and losses, and this acceptance is part of growing old. At this stage of life, we develop "ego integrity" and a sense of wisdom. We begin to tune in frequently to the inner voice of our "wise self, and we listen to it."

Mature adults who have successfully traversed the other seven developmental stages, develop the peak of adjustment, which Erikson termed *integrity*. Elder adults are independent, have found one or more well-defined roles in life, and have developed individual self-concepts with which they are content. Elder adults can be intimate without strain, and they are proud of what they have created—children and grandchildren, work, art, music, and a legacy for the future generations.

Conversely, elder adults who did not successfully navigate one or more of the earlier developmental stages may view their lives with disgust or despair. Adults in this final life stage need to look back on their own lives and feel a sense of fulfillment and meaning. Again, those who don't, or can't, may feel a sense of despair and depression; they may even dread their own death. They may also feel that it is too late to change their lives or themselves. These individuals frequently talk about having a lot of unfinished business; they resist change, and they fear the unknown.

Let's take a moment to look at how this affects those grandparents simultaneously dealing with the challenges of this final stage of life *and* who are raising their grandchildren.

In fact, parenting your grandchildren may reverse your psychological, emotional, and social momentum back to Erikson's seventh stage of development, "generativity versus stagnation." When this happens, part of the challenge involves the grandparents adapting to the demands of both stages (7 and 8), as well as to the demands of the stages that their grandchildren are in. This is no small task! Hopefully, this information will deepen your understanding of your feelings and experiences.

Here are some questions to consider:

- What happened to the part of you that was ready to retire when you made the decision to parent your grandchildren?

- What had you anticipated experiencing and enjoying during these later years of life that you then had to give up in order to raise your grandchildren?

- What activities are you engaged in on behalf of your grandchildren that you thought were part of the past?

- Have you returned to work in order to earn additional money to better manage the financial responsibilities?

- Do you find that you must engage in school activities on behalf of your grandchildren, or that you must drive them to and from various appointments and lessons on a regular basis?

Based on the answers to these questions, can you see that you have one foot in each of two different life stages? What a challenge this is! Yet, the many grandparents interviewed gave similar, consistently admirable responses to the following questions:

1. **How do you get through a day, let alone a month or a year?** "You do whatever it takes."

2. **How are you managing financially?** "Well, we are using our retirement money to pay the additional expenses." Or, "Grandpa went back to work."

3. **What will you do in the future as that money decreases?** "We'll figure it out then."

4. **How do you manage on a fixed budget?** "You learn to shop the sales; you know when different items are on sale during the month; you learn to do without."

5. **How is your energy level?** "Well, at 60, it's not what it was at thirty-five! But you get through it."

All the parenting grandparents interviewed, to a person—no matter their culture, gender, or age—basically said the same thing: "You do what you have to do. It's all about the kids. They have to be with family, not strangers." Everything takes a back seat to raising your grandchildren, plain and simple. The sacrifices you make, and the challenges you face, are huge.

The following story (begun in chapter 4) incorporates information from the previous chapter on developmental stages 1 through 7. It also addresses the challenges faced by grandparents who, while in their own final developmental life phase (stage 8), find themselves "pulled back" to the tasks of the previous phase (stage 7) because they are raising their grandchildren. This story focuses on the adjustment issues of the grandparents, not just the grandchildren.

> Hanna, age seventy-five, is raising two grandchildren, Brandon, who is currently thirteen, and Billy, who is eleven. Hanna, who was a widow, remarried fourteen years ago. Her second husband, Jack, is seventy-three years-old. Hanna raised six children of her own, and, with the exception of her son, Jon (Brandon and Billy's dad), all her children are doing well, gainfully employed, and raising their own children (Hanna's eighteen other grandchildren).
>
> Brandon and Billy came to Hanna because their drug-addicted parents could not, and did not, support or care for their boys. The boys' biological mother, Amy, is now in prison for prostitution and for selling and using drugs. Their biological father, Jon, was just released from jail, sleeps in cars, and is pretty much unavailable to his children.
>
> Brandon had been sleeping in a car with his biological parents when they came to Hanna to ask if she and Jack would "just take Brandon." At the time he was ten months old. Brandon had lived with his grandparents for three years when Amy and Jon asked Hanna and Jack to raise Billy, as well. He was eleven months old when he came to live with his grandparents.
>
> Hanna described raising the boys as "putting a strain on her marriage." Brandon and Billy were really step-grandchildren to Jack;

besides, in his mind, he and Hanna should have been "done raising kids." After some adjustment, Jack was able to accept Brandon; however, when Billy arrived, Hanna recalled how upset and angry Jack was.

At that time, Amy was not in jail, but, because she worked odd jobs, she was hard to contact. Finally, Hanna did reach Amy, telling her that she had to take Billy back. As a result, Hanna felt tremendous stress, which she described as "being caught in the middle." She expressed experiencing considerable inner conflict about giving Billy back to Amy, but she also understood Jack's position. When they married, he had not bargained for being a parenting step-grandparent.

According to Hanna, when Amy finally came to get Billy, she just stood on Hanna's porch, telling her, "I don't want my son back." Hanna further described that she had never felt so enraged in her entire life. She told Amy, "Then you had better sign a piece of paper right now giving me guardianship of both boys. I'll take it to an attorney so we legalize everything."

When Hanna told Jack what had happened, and he saw how upset his wife was, Jack decided that he would help raise and support both Brandon and Billy. Jack openly shared how very frustrated he felt at that time, realizing that raising the boys would change his and Hanna's lives, as well as their marriage.

It is important to recognize, and not minimize, the heavy burden that a couple must take on and deal with when forced to revisit a phase of life that they thought was finished. For Hanna and Jack, this return to parenthood—caring for another generation—was even more complicated, because the boys were Jack's step-grandchildren. Added to all the emotional and psychological components was the financial one. Having completed the seventh developmental stage, "generativity versus stagnation," Jack and Hanna barely had begun to enjoy the "integrity" of their elder years, and the freedom and relaxed time that these years promised. They were not wealthy, but they had enough for their retirement needs. Now, as parenting grandparents, they had to pinch pennies in order to cover their expenses.

When older adults have to move backward to a previous stage of life—which they have neither prepared for nor voluntarily chosen to do—it is just as challenging an adjustment for them as it is for their grandchildren. Both grandparents and grandchildren find themselves needing to adjust to life circumstances that they did not choose and are not ready for. The significant difference is the wisdom and maturity that grandparents have accrued over the years, which gives them far more internal resources for coping with life's challenges than children, teens, or younger adults can have.

Jack struggled considerably in order to accept a responsibility that he genuinely believed was not his to take on. Jack's response was neither unusual nor difficult to understand. What was unusual was his openness and willingness to reveal and discuss his emotions.

The elder generation, for the most part, does not find it easy to share their emotions. But it is important for them to know that discussing emotions openly is healthy, and it offers the opportunity to gain deeper mutual understanding with our life partners and our other loved ones. It also helps us realize that we must grieve our losses—whether we have lost a loved one, a dream, an expectation, a way of being, or anything else that is important to us. We cannot truly accept what we have lost unless we have grieved for it. In a way, every loss is a small death.

For Jack, it was the loss of privacy, as well as the loss of freedom to live and retire as he and Hanna had planned, which included not having the responsibility of raising children. In the end, Jack did not want to lose his marriage; he also did not want to see Hanna so deeply pained and worried that Billy would be unsafe or end up in foster care.

Many of the grandparent couples interviewed demonstrated how difficult it was for them to talk about this dilemma. For some, refusing a home to their grandchildren is an impossible choice. However, that does not mean they feel no inner conflict; a part of them may wish the situation requiring that they raise their grandchildren could be otherwise—or that it had never happened at all. It is not abnormal or selfish to want the elder years to match your hopes and expectations—to enjoy the retirement you planned and saved for, to spend your time doing pleasurable things.

When the front door opens, and the grandchildren walk in because their parents can't or won't raise them, for many grandparents, the back door also opens, and dreams of leisure and retirement suddenly exit. This is a big loss for parenting grandparents, and much grief and frustration accompany it. Again, most parenting grandparents do not give voice to these feelings, but they still exist, usually just below the surface.

Jack and Hanna were doing everything they could to raise the boys well and to give them a safe and loving home. Understandably upset when they acknowledged that Jack might never be able to retire, both Hanna and Jack expressed how grateful they were for their good health. It allowed Jack to go back to work and Hanna to care for the boys full-time, essentially being a stay-at-home mom at age seventy-five.

Hanna has not been able to adopt Brandon and Billy, because, in their state, the biological parents have to sign the adoption papers, and both Jon and Amy refuse. They refuse to allow an adoption, and they also refuse to raise their children in a safe, responsible way.

This is a real catch-22 situation for grandparents; one that occurs far too frequently. The law does not always support grandparents' rights, even when circumstances beyond their control have forced them to raise their grandchildren. In fact, many grandparents are afraid to report that they are parenting their grandchildren for fear that social-service agencies will take the children away and place them in foster care.

Foster care does not always provide financial support to grandparents so they can care for their own grandchildren. It seems ironic, however, that they will pay for strangers to care for these children.

The Children's Defense Fund, the Child Welfare League of America, the American Association of Retired People (AARP), the National Committee of Grandparents for Children's Rights, Generations United, and the Brookdale Foundation are but a few of the national organizations advocating on behalf of parenting grandparents. They all have websites, and they seek support to help them influence federal and state legislators to change and redefine laws and regulations in order to ensure the provision of financial, legal, health, and mental-health services to those children raised by their grandparents.

Gentle Reminders

1. Traversing the final developmental phase (stage 8), "integrity versus despair," becomes more complicated for those elders raising their grandchildren.

2. Discussing emotions openly is healthy, and it offers the opportunity to gain deeper mutual understanding with our life partners and our other loved ones. It also helps us realize that we must grieve our losses when significant life events occur.

3. Many national organizations advocate for programs that will support parenting grandparents, so that they can more effectively raise their grandchildren. You can find many of these organizations on the web by searching for "parenting grandparents" or "kinship caregivers." Here are some excellent websites:

    •   Children's Defense Fund: www.childrensdefense.org

    •   Child Welfare League of America: www.cwla.org

- American Association of Retired People (AARP): www.aarp.org/relationships/grandparenting

- National Committee of Grandparents for Children's Rights: www.grandparentsforchildren.org

- Generations United: www.gu.org/OURWORK/grandfamilies.aspx

- Brookdale Foundation: www.brookdalefoundation.org/RAPP/rapp.html

PART II: GRANDPARENTS' TRANSITION CHALLENGES

As you begin to raise your grandchildren, new life realities may leave you in shock. This shock may show up physically, in the form of new aches and pains, higher blood pressure, insomnia, and even shortness of breath, among other symptoms. Mentally and emotionally, it may appear as poor concentration, problem-solving difficulties, memory loss, depression, and even confusion, at times, among other expressions.

Socially, grandparents who had very active schedules—spending time visiting friends, playing cards, golf, or even traveling with other couples—now may need or choose to withdraw from these social moments, either suddenly or gradually. This withdrawal may be a result of financial limitations, shame, fear of being judged or criticized, lack of energy, lack of time, etc. Regardless of the reason—and of whether it is a necessity or a choice—you must keep in mind that this withdrawal occurs at exactly the time when you need more support.

Parenting grandparents all reach the same single, quiet moment of realization: that what they'd planned, envisioned, or dreamed life would be, at this stage, has been shattered by circumstances beyond their control. Slowing down, relaxing more, working part-time instead of full time, or perhaps fully retiring and not working at all, playing with your grandchildren while they visit, and then smiling as they return home—all this has vanished. The phase of life when you were supposed to have time to just enjoy yourself—to make any remaining dreams come true, or at least enjoy your recollections—has just ended.

Williams Bridges, author of *Transitions*, refers to this stage as an *ending*. A *transition* is an internal adjustment to an external change or shift that we experience in life. Usually this is a result of something ending to which we've grown accustomed and a new way of being commencing.[18] But it is important to note that this new way of being is not something that we adapt to immediately.

Parenting grandparents all pass through a middle transition stage that I like to call the "chaotic zone." During this stage, you simply have not yet quite adjusted to all the changes, disappointments, losses, and new challenges—that is, to the unexpected or to the unpredictable—and all this leaves you in a state of confusion and fatigue.

During this stage, a lot of quiet suffering goes on internally, as you are overwhelmed by more "life" than you can handle. When interviewed, most grandparents shared that they kept this "chaotic middle stage" —and their complex feelings about being in it—to themselves. They did this partly because they did not want to burden their grandchildren, and partly because this internalization (or silence) is typical of the sixty-five-plus set, frequently called the "Silent Generation."

One of the best ways to move through this chaotic time is to establish routines for everyone in the family. Routines, schedules, and structured activities provide a sense of predictability and control. This sense of control lessens anxiety and worry, and it also strengthens our coping abilities. It even builds our confidence, and we begin to feel more competent.

Also, it is important to lean on your strengths. If you are an organized individual, use your organizational skills to cope with the adjustments and readjustments that you are required to make. If you are a person who needs time to think and sort things out, give yourself the quiet time you need to "process," so that you can make good decisions and solve problems. If you are blessed with good energy, make sure you stay active: exercise, meditate, and walk, so that you feel refreshed and vital, and also so that you stimulate your "feel good" hormones and brain endorphins.

Be assured that this chaotic middle stage of your transition will pass; as it does, you will find yourself embracing your new beginning, which is the third and final stage of any transition. You will recognize this new beginning because clarity will replace your confusion, your fatigue will lessen, you will experience a modicum of control, and some degree of predictability will return.

One of the concerns expressed by many of the parenting grandparents interviewed was the amount of judgment and criticism they had to confront from the outside world, including some of their old friends. Many spoke of the criticism they received early on in their transition to becoming parents to their grandchildren. One of the most frequent comments was: "Why are you taking your grandchildren when your own adult child has so many problems? What makes you think you can do a better job raising your grandchildren?"

Another judgment is that parenting grandparents are either "enablers" or "rescuers," and that they should let their adult children manage their own problems. But grandparents' universal response to that was: "I am not about to let anything bad happen to my grandkids, no matter what you call me." Parenting grandparents singularly devote themselves to ensuring that their grandchildren are safe and loved—and that their grandchildren *feel* safe and loved, which gives them a sense of both security and belonging to a family. All this gives an essential message to your grandchildren: They matter, they are visible, they are important, and, most of all, they are loved.

One of the options I recommend for new parenting grandparents is to join a grandparent support group. Search on the Internet for "AARP" and "grandparents," (www.aarp.com/grandparents) and several resources will come up, including one entitled "A State Fact Sheet for Grandparents and Other Kinship Caregivers." Searching for "parenting grandparents" or "kinship caregivers" will also yield several resources, as previously mentioned. Don't let yourself be, or feel, alone or isolated as you do the sacred, noble work of raising your grandchildren! Join a support group of like-minded grandparents helping each other become parents again. AARP's State Fact Sheets will help you locate support groups for parenting grandparents in your state.

If we look beneath the surface of the many ways in which parenting grandparents cope, we will appreciate the levels of adaptation required. Many grandparents are part of cultures where the norm is that grandparents raise their grandchildren; as a result, this is expected, anticipated, and predictable. Despite this cultural pattern, the challenges of raising your grandchildren remain and so do the associated stressors.

For some unexpected parenting grandparents, the change from being grandparents to becoming parents was sudden, unanticipated, and unpredictable, and so it left you in a state of disbelief, even shock or dismay. For you there is the additional strain of feeling stunned and suddenly overwhelmed. These situations, more often than not, were precipitated by an event, such as sudden death, sudden arrest and incarceration, illness, unemployment, etc.

For other grandparents, the change was gradual, and so it became predictable at some point before it actually happened. The chronicity of slow change may leave you feeling "anticipatory" grief or anxiety. In other words, you might begin to realize what is coming, and what is about to happen, and then you anticipate the event and all the associated emotions before that event even occurs.

Whether the shift from being a grandparent to being a parenting grandparent was sudden or gradual, the grandparents interviewed described feeling a heavy cloud of responsibility and grief as they took their grandchildren into their homes. Again, let's emphasize that, in managing the additional responsibilities that raising your grandchildren demands, you also transition from the role of grandparent to that of parent. This is a loss for both you and your grandchildren. Yesterday, you were an angel of understanding, wisdom, patience, generosity, and playfulness. Today, you must set rules and expectations, and, once again, be a disciplinarian. You are not nearly as much fun as a parent as you are a grandparent, nor are you as patient.

Yet again, you can see why the work of parenting grandparents is so sacred and so noble. It asks you to lift yourself up to a place of understanding, endurance, and faith, which you otherwise would not experience. It requires you to dig deep, down into your very soul, in order to find the necessary resolve, strength, fortitude, and resilience to manage all the complex layers of responsibility that you now have, as well as all the associated emotions. As you find that resolve within yourself, you teach your grandchildren to find the same within themselves.

Knowing what to expect as you navigate the necessary transitions may be helpful to both you and your grandchildren. Your adaptation to the new family environment, and its new roles, is physical and behavioral in the beginning. You make new schedules; you establish new routines; perhaps you rearrange furniture and readjust rooms; you shop for food differently; you set up appointments around the kids' schedules; and so forth. These types of adjustments help everyone cope with the psychological and emotional adaptations that quickly follow.

We all miss our old routines and patterns, and the predictability that they brought. Both you and your grandchildren may dislike your new routines because they are unfamiliar; they require new thinking, new planning, and new behaviors. All of this is completely natural and normal! In time, these new patterns will begin to feel natural, and predictability will return to your lives. But it will take time. Generally, the physical adjustment is shorter than the emotional and psychological one. The physical adjustment can happen in a month or two; the emotional and psychological adjustment could take as long as one to two years. The length of time is based on whether the shift from being grandparents to parents was expected or unexpected, voluntary or involuntary, sudden or gradual, meaning that you did not see any other choice but to raise your grandchildren.

Another transition that you must make as parenting grandparents is managing your own reactions to what has happened to the parents of your grandchildren—that is, your own adult child(ren). You must face and learn to cope with at least two levels of responses as you begin raising your grandchildren: managing your own internal responses *and* managing your grandchildren's, or helping them manage their own if they are mature enough, chronologically and developmentally, to do so. (Chapter 6 will discuss this in detail.)

The grandparents interviewed displayed consistent and deeply moving resilience and courage. They grieved the loss of their own adult child— whether it was to physical death or to an emotional/psychological "death"—and, in any and all circumstances, this was an upsetting loss. The grief a parent feels at the death of a child of any age needs no further elaboration. The grief a parent feels because of emotional or psychological "death" is much harder to describe. The story that follows shows a counterpoint of these two types of grief. (Chapter 6 will describe more of this story.)

One of the grandfathers interviewed, Elliott, described that his daughter was killed instantly in an auto accident as she was driving to pick up her son, Gregory, from school. Gregory's father, Adam, was so devastated by the sudden death of his wife that he became emotionally and psychologically absent to his son. Some part of Adam died when his wife died. He was unable to function and carry out his responsibilities as a father. In fact, he never talked to Gregory about what happened to his mother. Gregory's older sisters finally told him that their mom had died in an auto accident. Life as they had known it permanently ended for Elliott, his son-in-law, and his grandchildren. And, while the physical death of Elliott's daughter brought great anguish to him and his family, his son-in-law's emotional and psychological absence was far more demoralizing and distressing.

For Gregory, although his father was physically present, his emotional and psychological absence was a kind of "death." Although the rest of the family felt it, this was especially devastating for Gregory and his older sisters. Sadly, Gregory's father remained unavailable to his son, and so Gregory went to live with his grandfather, who has been raising him for the last five years.

It is important for you, as parenting grandparents, to utilize the unique wisdom that you have accrued throughout your years of life experiences. You are not the same person as a grandparent that you were as a parent. In most instances, this is a good thing. You are wiser, more insightful, and you understand what matters in life—and what does not matter. As a grandparent, you can offer your grandchildren what you could not offer your own children when you parented them. As a parent, you were too young to be wise; besides, you were invested in your children in a different way. Perhaps you needed them to achieve, to get good grades, to be competitive in sports, music, dance, etc. You may want similar things for your grandchildren, but it is more important to you that they understand how unique they are; that they determine their own core values and beliefs; that they be true to themselves, by learning how to live their lives in a way that expresses those values and beliefs.

As grandparents, we all see mistakes as opportunities to grow. We realize that the "perfect parent" and the "perfect child" do not exist. We don't need our grandkids to be straight-A students; we need them to be contributors to life—we need them to be well-rounded, thoughtful, playful, and, most important, true to who they really are. As parenting grandparents, you have an even greater ability to inculcate these essentials in your grandchildren.

The bottom line is: Even though you have become parents again, don't disregard the "life valuables" you have acquired with age. Utilize them as you parent your grandchildren, and they will come to realize that the treasures you share with them will enrich their lives in ways no one—neither they, you, their parents, nor anyone else—could have imagined.

Gentle Reminders

1. A *transition* is an internal adjustment to an external change or shift that we experience in life when something to which we've grown accustomed ends, and a new way of being commences.

2. It is important to understand that transitions are about our internal shifts, and so the adaptations that we need to make will require patience and self-awareness. These shifts are uneven and can feel chaotic at times, especially in the beginning; but, as routines and new expectations become familiar, these "bumps in the road" do smooth out.

3. Generally, the physical adjustment is shorter in duration than the emotional and psychological one. The physical adjustment can happen in a month or two; the emotional and psychological adjustment could take one to two years.

4. Be sure to utilize the unique wisdom that you have accrued throughout your years of life experiences to help you cope as you raise your grandchildren.

6

UNDERSTANDING AND MANAGING POWERFUL EMOTIONS

PART I: THE EMOTIONAL AND PSYCHOLOGICAL IMPACT OF ABANDONMENT

Many parenting grandparents interviewed across the country talked about how hard it is to help grandchildren manage intense emotions and psychological turmoil. Unfortunately, many of your grandchildren have been abused, neglected, or traumatized in some way. This chapter will help you understand the dynamics behind the difficult and challenging behaviors that some of your grandchildren display.

"Mercurial and volatile"; "given to bouts of tears and fits of rage"; "guarded"; "withdrawn"; "uncommunicative"; "fearful"—these phrases and words are but a few of the ones that may describe traumatized children and teens. Do any of these words describe your grandchildren? Any tiny pebble in the road of your grandchildren's lives can become a boulder rolling down a steep hill, picking up speed and intensity. Episodes of confusion, commotion, and loss of control can easily emerge in children and teens who come from backgrounds of abuse, neglect, or trauma.

Many grandparents interviewed shared a similar concern: the inconsistent presence of the grandchildren's parents in their lives. Some of the situations described included parents showing up impulsively and without notice; parents promising to visit on a certain day, and then not showing up and not calling; parents visiting while under the influence of alcohol, drugs, or both; parents making, and breaking, all sorts of promises. In most of the situations described, these experiences devastated grandchildren of all ages, and understandably so.

These parents—whether biological or adoptive—display chaotic, confusing, and rejecting behavioral patterns, which psychology refers to as *push-and-pull patterns*. These patterns are major stressors that contribute considerable instability in situations that are already fragile. Push-and-pull patterns are contradictions in the messages we all give to each other, and these contradictions create uncertainty. When children and teens receive contradictory messages, it often results in feelings of helplessness and hopelessness, especially if this continues for a long time. Children and teens don't have the mental and emotional resources to make sense of the mixed or contradictory messages that they receive from their parents; as a result, their parents' irregular and erratic behaviors leave these children and teens feeling abandoned and rejected.

One of the biggest push-and-pull signals occurs when children hear the hurtful and critical voice of the parent: "If you did what I told you, you would not have messed up so badly." Regardless of the parenting intention, children hear far more than a corrective message. Consider this message from the children's perspective: They hear and believe that not only did they make a mistake, but they also must be incompetent, and that is why they "messed up so badly." In short, they hear judgment that they were disobedient, yet they are still dependent on the parents' direction in order to learn. All this can leave children of any age feeling stupid, hurt, and angry.

The paragraph above describes the "push." The children in this situation feel "pushed away." The "pull" occurs later, when a parent says: "Why are you acting so hurt? Don't be such a baby! You know I love you. Come here and let me hug you."

Children in this situation receive a rapid-fire series of contradictory messages: First, negating their feelings of hurt or anger, and then judging them for "acting like a baby" or being otherwise inadequate; after which, they immediately receive another contradictory message that the parent loves them and wants a hug to display affection. However, such children—upset and confused—frequently are not ready for a hug at that moment; they are experiencing hurtful emotions, which the parent has effectively minimized, generating even more confusion in these children.

To further complicate the situation, children who refuse the hug, may receive further judgment or criticism, and perhaps verbal---or even physical—abuse. Yet, children who accept the hug, despite not wanting it, bury their real feelings and experience the entire transaction as inauthentic. Regardless, repeated events like this can mark the beginning of a push-and-pull pattern that these children are likely to take into adulthood. It would not be unusual to see this pattern repeated in their own intimate relationships with partners and friends—and, eventually, with their own children.

One of the most common push-and-pull patterns mentioned by the parenting grandparents who were interviewed, was one where the grandchildren's parents would tell the kids: "I know you were upset and afraid when I left, but it was just for a few days. Come over here and let me hug you. I can't believe you are this upset. You know I love you." Here, the parent minimizes their own aberrant behaviors—showing no accountability for them. This leaves children feeling self doubt, confusion, mistrust, and anger; often, whether immediately or over time, these kids turn that anger inward, which may lead to depression or acting-out.

Not allowing people to experience their true emotions—or even just minimizing what they feel—leaves both children and adults feeling bewildered. It can make us freeze where we can't think or respond, take flight, fight, or believe that something is "wrong" with how we feel. It can even lead to belligerent attitudes and behaviors.

This is difficult enough for adults who generally have the internal resources to combat this. In children, who have not yet developed such resources, unless they have someone in their lives to tell or show them otherwise, these kids will reach the inevitable conclusion that "It is not okay to feel." When they feel unsafe to express their authentic emotions, children begin to mask, conceal, or act them out—none of which is an appropriate coping response that will serve your grandchildren, short- or long-term.

As parenting grandparents, it is important for you not to allow such communication between your grandchildren and their biological (or adoptive) parents, if it exists. It is also important for you to set limits and boundaries for your grandchildren's parents in terms of what is, or is not, acceptable behaviors. This can be hard for you because the limitations and boundaries set are frequently aimed at your own adult children, which may ignite internal, unresolved, emotional responses in you—and in them. It is also difficult because you may end up needing to seek guardianship in order to have the legal right to protect your grandchildren.

In a push-and-pull pattern, children or teens may feel rejected or, worse yet, abandoned. The parent's momentary acceptance, which is always conditional, may follow this. In such situations, children get two distinctly different messages. After a time, these children will feel like they can't make mistakes and can't be authentic with their emotions, for fear that the parent will criticize them or disappear. These children or teens may believe the parent left because of something they did or said. A manipulative quality to the matter emerges, leaving the children feeling victimized. Push-and-pull patterns are crazy-making behaviors and, consequently, should not be tolerated!

Moreover, children and teens caught in long term push-and-pull patterns can develop one or more of the following reactions: hypersensitivity, neediness, withdrawal, placating behaviors, excessive cautiousness, a poor sense of reality, blaming behaviors, violent acting out toward self or others, or an "I don't care" attitude. Push-and-pull patterns have a high emotional cost, causing those caught up in them to lose the ability to trust—and also to lose or damage the all-important sense of self—while trying to adjust to an external environment that is unpredictable, confusing, and disappointing. The repetition of this pattern can lead children and teens to feel unloved, rejected, abandoned, and traumatized.

This kind of wounding affects not only the grandchildren but the grandparents, as well. In fact, many grandparents interviewed described significant feelings of guilt, shame, anger, regret, and self-blame when their own adult children were absent because of addictions, crime, promiscuity, divorce, etc. The pain in the eyes of these grandmothers and grandfathers was evident as they described having to deal with their adult children's deviant behaviors. Grandparents said that their friends, neighbors, and people in general would label their adult children as "lazy, irresponsible, selfish, manipulative, and self-serving," among other judgmental descriptions.

But worst of all are the comments made by others about these grandparents' own lack of parenting skills—that is, how others judge and blame them for the "sins" and mistakes of their adult children. Although previously mentioned, it bears repeating because so many grandparents interviewed described hearing this same judgment so frequently: "You messed up raising your own child, why do you think you can raise your grandchildren?"

Feeling vulnerable, fatigued, and overwhelmed, grandparents can go into "overload" as a result of the assumptions and judgments about their own supposed parental mistakes, combined with the inference that they will repeat those mistakes with their grandchildren. Usually, these assumptions, judgments, and inferences are unfair and unwarranted, but it still takes a lot of inner strength to manage such harsh criticism. Try to remember and focus on the reason why you have taken on this sacred and noble task: your grandchildren. Your love for them, and theirs for you, matters far more than anything else.

It takes a huge capacity for love to persevere after your life has flipped 180 degrees from what you expected it would be at this stage—that is, prior to your grandchildren coming into your home. It also takes a lot of patience, understanding, and energy to work, support, and care for your grandchildren, many of whom are troubled and traumatized by the absence of their parents. Finally, it takes a lot of resilience and strength to acknowledge and accept the problems or loss of your own adult child.

It is important for us to understand there is a story for every adult son or daughter who is unable to mature or grow into responsible adults and parents. Interestingly, many of these troubled individuals have siblings who are managing life quite well. Does some biological predisposition exist that makes one child able to cope better than another? Do environmental influences exist that negatively impact one child more than the other? Is it each child's constitutional makeup and character that provides the deciding factor of how he or she "turns out"? No one has the answer to these questions. Psychology offers differing viewpoints, and the actual "answer" might be components from any combination of these questions, or from all of them together. However, one thing is sure: All these questions weigh heavily on the minds of many parenting grandparents.

One grandparent from Illinois said this when interviewed: "I cried and cried, and then I cried some more, until I ran out of tears. That's when I finally stopped crying. But I haven't stopped worrying about my daughter. I haven't stopped blaming myself, and I haven't stopped wondering where she is, if she's all right, and if she's even still alive."

This deep torment is present daily for many parenting grandparents; yet, every day, they have to get out of bed, and push through the heaviness they feel so that they can be present and available for their grandchildren.

When grandchildren experience pain, grandparents experience pain. Children who experience the pain of abandonment—whether as a result of death, desertion neglect, or some other trauma—find it hard to become optimistic about life. Take heart: It is hard, but it is not impossible. It is also hard to move beyond feeling plagued and overwhelmed by continual messages of not being "good enough," not being "lovable." Again, take heart: It is hard, but it is not impossible.

While issues related to abandonment always leave a psychological and emotional wound, children experience abandonment in different ways. Some children encounter it because of the death of one or both parents. The pain resulting from illness or accident-related abandonment hurts but, over time, the realization that the parent did not want to die but could not prevent the illness, accident, etc., can soften the pain and loss for children and teens. Where loving relationships existed prior to the loss, the pain and grief for the lost parent is certainly no less deep, but, over time, it may give way to the comfort of fond memories and the abiding feelings of having been loved, cared for, and wanted. As parenting grandparents in such situations, you can effectively reinforce this, and help your grandchildren overcome the loss more quickly than they otherwise would be able to.

For example, let's return to the story of Gregory (chapter 5), whose mother was killed suddenly in an auto accident.

> Seven-year-old Gregory waited for his mother to pick him up after school, just as she did every day. He waited and waited, but his mother never came. Eventually, a neighbor came to pick up Gregory, and when he arrived home he was told by his grieving father that his mother was "gone." Eventually, Gregory's older sisters explained that their mother had been killed in an auto accident.

> Gregory cried for his mother for a long time, and he felt deep sadness. As he grew older, Gregory continued to miss his mother, and it was not until he was a young adult that he came to understand that his mother did not choose to leave him. Finally, he was able to find some solace in the warm memories he had of his mother.

Another kind of abandonment that leaves deep and permanent wounds is that which occurs when parents are physically alive, but absent from their children's life. Let us again consider Gregory's situation. Following his mother's death, Gregory experienced a second abandonment from his father's emotional absence. This resulted because Gregory's father, Adam, could not handle the sudden death of his wife.

> *Devastated, Adam became permanently distant, noncommunicative, depressed, and emotionally unavailable to Gregory. Adam had several unsuccessful short-term marriages following the death of his children's mother. He was no longer able to handle his responsibilities as a father.*

> *Their maternal grandparents took Gregory and his three older sisters to live with them, and they raised the children until they were grown.*

During such a tragic time, the children receive a lot of attention, and understandably so. However, the grandparents also need attention and support at this time. Gregory's grandfather, Elliott, related how especially difficult it was for him and his wife to mourn the death of their own daughter, while trying to support and raise their four grandchildren. If you are a grandparent grieving the loss of your adult child—for whatever reason—seek grief counseling, so that you can address your own needs while you simultaneously bear the responsibility for meeting your grandchildren's needs.

> *Initially, Gregory's reaction to his losses manifested in insomnia, excessive fears, bedwetting, angry impulses, and clinging behaviors. This once loving, friendly, playful, and spontaneous child had become withdrawn, tentative, and cautious.*

This is only one example of the effects of abandonment on children. Furthermore, those effects, if not healed, can continue to have a negative impact on individuals well into adulthood.

Gregory experienced a double abandonment, and, long-term, his father's abandonment of him wounded him far more than his mother's. Although he grieved for his deceased mother for a long time, he did come to terms with it and was able to understand that his mother's death had been completely outside her control. The abandonment and rejection he felt from his father, Adam, was vastly different. As Gregory grew older, he simply could not make sense of the fact that his father, who was alive, would not raise him—and never even came to visit. Gregory's abandonment issues because of Adam's absence, which the son saw as voluntary on the father's part, were far more challenging and complex to deal with than his feelings related to his mother's death.

With the emotional and physical abandonment of his father, Gregory became more and more confused and angry, which led to self-doubt about his own worthiness. "If my own father doesn't want me, maybe I'm not worth loving," is what children in this situation are prone to think. This self-doubt carried forward into Gregory's teen years and young adulthood, and it negatively affected his decisions about the women he dated and the friends he chose.

Once again, we see how an event early in life—in this case at the age of seven—impacted the child, Gregory, all the way through his young adulthood. As a young adult, Gregory had a hard time getting close to friends, and even to the women he dated. He harbored a constant fear of abandonment. To reveal his deepest thoughts and feelings to another person was to risk the pain of rejection or abandonment. Gregory was not willing to take that risk, and so his relationships were superficial and casual.

Yet Gregory wanted more from his relationships with others. Unable to experience any kind of intimacy, Gregory sought counseling. With the support of a caring counselor, Gregory made rapid progress. He was able to see how his anxiety and fear interfered with his ability to risk being himself in his romantic relationships and friendships. In therapy, he was able to confront his fears and old wounds. As he grew more confident, Gregory made new friends with whom he had deeper, more authentic relationships; likewise, the women he chose to date were less needy and more mature. Once he addressed and healed his unresolved abandonment wounds, Gregory was able to move beyond isolation to experience true intimacy in his significant relationships.

An important impact of abandonment is the constant anxiety and fear that we carry within us as a result. It is so constant, in fact, that children and teens begin to see life through apprehensive and uneasy lenses. Fear distorts reality, and this causes us to mistrust others, even those who have stood by us and raised us. Grandchildren may seemingly challenge their grandparents over and over again, to ensure their safety, making sure they can trust they won't be abandoned again.

Because of the internal anxiety and fear that so many of your grandchildren experience, their need for approval, recognition, attention, and love may seem exaggerated. As parenting grandparents, you may notice that your grandchildren's emotional appetite is insatiable. They may display this in a variety of ways: Some disguise this emotional appetite, acting as if they don't really care if they receive attention or not, even though they hover around you constantly. Others may make themselves extraordinarily helpful or indispensable hiding their deep fear of more rejection; still others may become complainers and critics of everything that is happening. Children are brilliant at getting attention, whether it's positive or negative. This variety of responses relates to your grandchildren's deep need to ensure that they are not rejected or abandoned again—especially not by you.

Rejection and abandonment can leave a big emotional hole in children and teens, and it often seems that nothing can ever fill up that hole. As these children grow into adulthood, this emotional hole can contribute to masking behaviors, where individuals hide their pain to keep from being seen as fragile or vulnerable. Often, this masking is the core cause of addictions, which serve to numb emotional pain and suffering. It also prevents these individuals from experiencing true intimacy and healthy relationships in their adult years.

As the parenting grandparent, you may have to confront and deal with all of this. This book offers you a variety of ways to cope with the emotional and behavioral challenges that some of your grandchildren may present.

To manage the issues of abandonment and rejection many grandchildren suffer due to the loss or absence of one or both parents, grandparents must first identify and acknowledge the specific problems that their grandchildren are experiencing. Education and information about the impact of abandonment on children of various ages can be found on the Internet, in books and magazines, and in local seminars offered by social-service agencies that offer assistance for children and families.

If you are worried about your grandchildren's behaviors, consult a child specialist as soon as possible. Child and family agencies provide some services to the uninsured, and can frequently assist you in obtaining insurance coverage for both medical and mental-health problems. As mentioned earlier, both AARP and the Children's Defense Fund, both headquartered in Washington, DC, offer state-by-state resources for grandparents raising their grandchildren. They also are helpful in identifying grandparent support groups on a state-by-state basis, and these grandparent support groups really know what is available in your state, city, town, or community. (For a list of websites, see chapter 5, part 1, Gentle Reminders.)

Frequent contact with your grandchildren's teachers, school counselors, or social workers is vital. As parenting grandparents, you need to make your grandchildren's schools part of their support system. You may also want to keep their schools informed about any treatment interventions and services your grandchildren may be receiving. When possible, arrange for one of the professionals working with your grandchildren to become the coordinator for all the professionals and agencies involved with maintaining your grandchildren's well-being. This will ensure a coordinated effort of support for your grandchildren.

Also, as parenting grandparents, you will need to offer consistent, predictable, and loving messages to your grandchildren, reassuring them of their importance, their goodness, and their safety—and your unconditional love for them. Structured activities and schedules will help make things predictable for your grandchildren, which, in turn, will support their sense of security and sense of belonging—both of which will help them form a positive sense of self. Safety and security, as mentioned in previous chapters, are primary needs for human beings; but, for your grandchildren, because of their situation, this is the highest priority.

Taking time for games, sports, and play is important for several reasons. First, playing together is good bonding time. It will serve to relax inner tensions, as play and laughter help release "feel good" hormones in the brain. Play benefits both grandparents *and* grandchildren!

Parenting grandparents need some light moments, just as the grandchildren do. Given the chaos in your lives, you will only have time for relaxation and respite if you make the time, and plan for it. If you schedule this time into your week, just like other appointments, your message to your grandchildren will be: This time is *important!*

Many grandparents interviewed described how hard it is to play and laugh, when life feels so filled with responsibility and worry. But pushing through the resistance is a must—not only because you need and deserve some relaxation, but also because you are a role model for your grandchildren, and this shows them the importance of making the time to de-stress. If you hold this expectation for yourselves, it will be easier to hold it for your grandchildren, and they will be more accommodating. Over time, it is important that grandchildren make this their own priority. Words reinforced by behaviors and beliefs are wonderful ways to teach your grandchildren, and this is also important to their well-being.

You might want to consider joining or starting a grandparents-raising-their-grandchildren support group. The meetings of these groups offer incredible moments filled with laughter, wisdom, tears, support, information, resource advocacy, understanding, respite, and, most important, heart. No individuals on this planet express more heart, sacrifice, and love than parenting grandparents do toward their grandchildren! This is sacred, noble work. It's crucial that you, as parenting grandparents, find and give yourselves the support you deserve. When you give this to yourselves, ultimately, your grandchildren receive it, too.

Gentle Reminders

1. Children being raised by their grandparents frequently must deal with issues of abandonment, rejection, and/or neglect caused by the loss of one or both parents.

2. Grandparents need to support each other, and their grandchildren, as they adapt to the multiple changes and transitions that they face while raising their grandchildren.

3. Both grandparents and grandchildren experience considerable losses, and it is not unusual for both to feel deep grief and sadness for an extended period of time.

4. In situations where adult children engage in deviant behaviors, and exhibit erratic, confusing behavior or inconsistent contact with their children—your grandchildren—you must set firm boundaries and limits in order to protect your grandchildren. Anything that jeopardizes your grandchildren's safety and security is not acceptable.

5. The very act of your raising your grandchildren communicates to them that they are important, they matter, they are worthy, and they are loved.

6. It is critical for grandparents to educate themselves about available resources, and to utilize all the support available for both themselves and their grandchildren.

7. Starting, or finding and joining a grandparent support group is important to your well-being, and, ultimately, to your grandchildren's, too.

8. Relaxing and taking time to de-stress is more than important, it is vital.

PART II: THE BODY'S RESPONSE TO STRESSFUL EMOTIONS

Many of your grandchildren may experience constant, overwhelming emotions, which can be confusing and chaotic—for both them and you, as parenting grandparents. At times, these "ups and downs" may feel like "crazy-making" to you. These intense emotions may cause both you and your grandchildren to experience chronic activation of the body's fight-flight-freeze hormones primarily triggered during crisis situations.

Because so many of your grandchildren come from backgrounds of abuse, neglect, or loss, most likely they have experienced chronic activation of the fear-alarm system, along with its "fight, flight, or freeze" responses. These are extreme responses, intended for activation only during crisis situations. When they are overutilized on an ongoing basis, the part of the brain near the brain stem is flooded with the hormones norepinephrine and cortisol, which provide the necessary energy to fight or flee. Numerous neurological researchers agree that we all need those chemicals for survival, but an excessive release of them on a too-frequent basis negatively affects the brain, causing it to malfunction.[19]

Cortisol, one of the survival chemicals, rearranges the distribution of our energy to assist with prolonged stress. Bremner (2002) states that cortisol increases our heart rate, raises our blood pressure, supplies more serum glucose, provides oxygen and strength to the brain and muscles, and enhances blood coagulation ability, to name a few of the essential physiological changes we need to survive in extreme circumstances.[20] An excessive production of cortisol however, can lead to adrenal fatigue.

Two of the most common complaints grandparents mentioned during their interviews was feeling fatigue and lethargy. The stress of being a parenting grandparent requires you make time for relaxation to ensure your health and well-being.

Bremner explains that elevated levels of the stress hormone cortisol can damage the hippocampus, which is the area of the brain involved in learning and memory. Elevated cortisol also affects moods, which leads to depression and feelings of fatigue. Again, this is why it is so critical for parenting grandparents to manage not only the stress levels of their grandchildren, but their own stress levels as well.

As they now live with you, many grandchildren no longer are in unsafe home environments, but their earlier traumas are set in their memories— especially the ones that they experienced frequently. This leaves them in a state of constant hypervigilance; these children and teens seem to always be "on guard," tense about potential and unseen dangers.

Depending upon the circumstances, your grandchildren may have had to face one or more risk factors before they came to live in the safe environment of your home. The list of potential risk factors includes, but is not limited to:

- Exposure to drugs, alcohol, and/or Sexually Transmitted Diseases (STDs) while in utero (leading to addicted and/or gravely ill newborns/infants)

- Malnutrition of the pregnant mother

- Cigarettes, caffeine, alcohol, and/or various types drugs (both illegal substances and abuse of prescription drugs) used by the pregnant mother

- Absence of prenatal care

- Premature birth

- Birth complications

- Abuse, neglect, trauma, and/or abandonment

At-risk infants and children lose several important life gifts, not the least of which is trust. Trust involves children's inner sense of their own worth and preciousness, a safe attachment to a reliable, trustworthy caregiver, and a sense that they are wanted and deserve to be well cared for. Instead, too many at-risk children have received these messages: "I don't like you," which is the message of abuse; "you don't exist," which is the message of neglect; "I don't want you," which is the message of abandonment. In all three cases, children bury shame in their core, where their sense of self-worth should reside.

Young children (under the age of ten) who have experienced such turbulent histories are at high risk for an excessive production of cortisol and adrenaline. Because they have pumped these hormones so hard and for so long, they may experience adrenal burn-out at young ages. The overproduction of adrenaline is associated with withdrawn, depressed, anxious, fearful, and/or other internalizing behaviors, which are also known as "acting in" behaviors. As these children approach their preadolescent and teen years, they may experience *adrenal depletion,* which is associated with aggression, delinquency, and/or other externalizing behaviors, which are also known as "acting out" behaviors."[21]

The overproduction of stress hormones is accompanied by the underproduction of calming brain chemicals, such as serotonin, which is the master regulator of the brain. Medical specialists consider serotonin the "feel good" hormone of the brain, because it urges the release of endorphins, which foster a lasting sense of well-being, as well as sustained feelings of joy, happiness, contentment, and calmness. Deficits in serotonin are associated with a host of mental and emotional disorders, including Post-Traumatic Stress Disorder (PTSD), Obsessive-Compulsive Disorder (OCD), Bi-Polar Disorder, Depression, Anxiety Disorder, Attention-Deficit Disorder, and many others.[22]

Both children and adults develop serotonin through several pathways: nutritious food; safe, affectionate, loving touch; an environment of "felt safety"; and healthy physical activity. The balance in the bodies and brains of children who receive attentive, nurturing care becomes the foundation for later mental health and emotional self-regulation. Later, as healthy children move through the developmental stages (*see* chapter 4), they are able to regulate themselves because of the cycle they experienced repeatedly during their formative years.

Even when healthy children experience a flood of stress hormones and neurotransmitters, as long as their parents or caregivers comfort and care for them, they will experience the gentle release of calming, healing, regulating neurotransmitters. Thus, they develop the brain regulation that becomes the foundation for later behavioral regulation. When someone hurts the feelings of children who received soothing when they needed it, even though they get upset, they are able to calm themselves; they can self-regulate.

In contrast, many children in your grandchildren's situation may never have experienced the calming cycle, or it may have occurred intermittently. Without the consistent experience of a nurturing calming cycle, these children are vulnerable to the neurochemicals in the brain associated with danger—and with the "fight, flight, or freeze" response.

These changes in brain development are important mechanisms that drive the appearance of mental illness. Reinforced by children's experience with early caregivers, these changes lead to the inability to trust, lack of attachment to a safe caregiver, overproduction of excitatory brain chemicals, and underproduction of serotonin and other calming brain chemicals. These are the mechanisms that actually drive mental illness in many children.[23] For more information and resources on this important topic, please visit the following website:

http://www.child.tcu.edu/Secondary%20Pages/Training_Articles.htm.

As you research and inform yourselves about managing your grandchildren's unique needs, remember some of these old-time, full-proof remedies to boost grandparents and grandchildren's immune and adrenal systems, as well as the feel-good hormones, like serotonin:

- Picnics

- Cuddling

- Spontaneous hugs

- Making ice-cream cones at home and eating them on the front porch together

- Baking cookies together

- Playing hide–and-seek outside on summer nights

- Playing "hot potato" with a real potato

- Sipping hot chocolate in front of the fireplace

- Jumping rope

- Playing flashlight tag

- Storytelling—sharing personal stories as well as made-up stories

- Playing charades or board games

Gentle Reminders

1. Push-and-pull patterns are contradictions in the messages we give to each other; these contradictions create uncertainty, in both children and adults. When children

receive contradictory messages, it often results in feelings of helplessness and hopelessness, if the contradictions continue for a long time.

2. Push-and-pull patterns are a major stressor for people, but especially children and teens, as these patterns contribute considerable instability in situations that are already fragile.

3. The overproduction of stress hormones is accompanied by the underproduction of calming brain chemicals, such as serotonin. Therefore, it is important that both grandparents and grandchildren find activities that not only reduce stress on a daily basis, but also raise the production of the feel-good hormones such as serotonin.

4. Utilize some of the tried-and-true, "sure to make you feel better" remedies to boost both yours and your grandchildren's adrenal and immune-systems. Time together playing, baking, storytelling, etc. is a time of poignant connection which will strengthen everyone's health and well-being.

7
COPING STRATEGIES FOR PARENTING GRANDPARENTS

The previous chapter provided a brief description of the chemistry of the body and mind. The purpose of this description was to alert you, as parenting grandparents, that the incredibly intense and strong emotions your grandchildren may display do have a physiological impact. This impact affects both the brain chemicals and adrenal hormones, which is to say that their emotions are not just verbal and behavioral in nature. The body, mind and spirit of each human being, together, form a "system." As a result, something occurring in one part of the system— whether positive or negative—automatically impacts the other parts of that system. Thus, we need to look at our children in their entirety or wholeness and, therefore, holistically.

The strategies and recommendations that follow are effective coping mechanisms because they reflect a holistic (healing of the body, mind and spirit) approach.

Looking for Patterns and Triggers

You may see two types of behavioral patterns in your grandchildren: externalizing, also called "acting out"; or, internalizing (turning inward), also, called "acting in." Both patterns need to be observed for very important reasons. Whether children "act out" their frustration by externalizing it, or "act in" their frustration by internalizing it, they do so because of overwhelming emotions that they are unable to handle and cope with. It is essential to remember that they do not "act out" or "act in" in order to make your life more challenging or difficult. Understanding the underlying reasons for their behaviors is of paramount importance.

"Acting out" looks like this: temper tantrums, yelling, throwing things, stamping feet, hitting or biting, name calling, slamming doors, fighting, being sarcastic, or exhibiting any other observable "oppositional" behaviors.

"Acting in" looks like this: pouting, withdrawing, not talking, isolating themselves, hiding, exhibiting passivity, spending long and aimless hours watching TV, avoiding things, being silent to "punish" you or others, or exhibiting any other observable inward behaviors which can also be considered oppositional.

The first thing parenting grandparents need to do when confronted by "acting out" or "acting in" behaviors is to understand that their grandchildren are experiencing a great deal of stress. Realizing these behaviors are not directed at you prevents you from taking any of it personally, which is very important. Your grandchildren are reacting from their memories of trauma, fear, or vulnerability. They struggle with deep-seated fear exaggerated by an inability to trust, and the combination makes them feel internally vulnerable and fragile.

One of the most important things you can do is to look for patterns that trigger your grandchildren's meltdowns. A *trigger* is any word, behavior, message, tone of voice, facial expression, body language, time of day or night, or other observable variable that sets off—or activates—a painful memory or experience. Some triggers to look for might include:

- Uncontrollable behaviors or emotional outbursts occurring at a certain time of the day or night. You can ask yourself what might have happened in the past during this particular time of day or night that would cause this extreme response.

- Overreaction to certain verbal or nonverbal cues, such as a specific tone of voice, facial expression, body language (e.g., the way you stand, or how physically close to your grandchildren you sit or stand), multiple noises, or other environmental distractions. (Ask yourself what might have occurred in the past that would link to any of these factors.)

- Overreaction to the sound of the wind, shadows in the room at night, too many people talking at the same time, background noise like television, music, traffic, etc. (Again, ask yourself what might have occurred in the past that would link to any of these factors.)

- Fatigue or hunger can create overreactions. Do your grandchildren get enough uninterrupted sleep? Do they eat healthy, nutritious foods at routine times? Or, do they fill up on foods with high sugar or carbohydrates, causing negative side effects as a result of spikes and drops of blood-sugar levels?

- Certain foods act like triggers, including: candy, cookies, diet drinks with aspartame, regular soda with high caffeine content (colas and Mountain Dew).

- Personality traits of certain peers and teachers may be triggers that overwhelm your grandchildren. What are your grandchildren's moods and behaviors like after school? Is homework a trigger? Homework assignments frequently trigger children who feel that they are not capable of or smart enough to successfully complete these assignments.

- Competition with siblings, cousins, or peers can create triggers for your grandchild.

- Certain expectations as to how your grandchildren "should" behave in specific circumstances can create triggers.

It can be very instructive to keep a journal to help you see any possible trigger patterns. Your observations need to include the interactions, events, and experiences that your grandchildren had prior to the "acting out" or "acting in" episode. Also, you want to note any changes that occur as a result of specific interventions that you and support professionals provide to your grandchildren. In essence, you want to note the causative factors, as well as whether they are patterns or isolated incidents; it is often easier to differentiate when you can review something in writing, rather than rely on your memory to recall the events and what precipitated them. You also want to notice the impact, positive or negative, of any coping strategies that you or others implement on behalf of your grandchildren. Pay close attention to the degree of success or frustration these strategies create.

Stated simply: What prevents your grandchildren's difficult behaviors from arising, and what does or doesn't work to resolve those behaviors when they occur?

"Use Your Words!"

Astute parents and grandparents encourage children to express their feelings and thoughts, telling them, "Use your words!" In some nursery and preschool programs, teachers communicate through sign language, which allows preverbal toddlers an avenue of expression. Encouraging little ones, as well as older children, to speak and share their thoughts and feelings allows them to verbalize what is upsetting them, instead of "acting out" or "acting in."

> Recently, my two-year-old granddaughter was upset because it was her naptime, and she was not ready to take a nap. When she started crying and fussing, her mother encouraged her to "use her words" to express her frustration. As they walked into my granddaughter's bedroom, she looked at her Mom and said: "And you have to _listen_ to my words Mommy!"

When children do in fact, "use their words," we must communicate we have heard them, even if the outcome is not always to their desire. What is important is teaching them an acceptable way to express their thoughts and emotions. By encouraging your grandchildren to use their words, you give them permission to express their feelings and to tell you what they need. This communicates another important message from you to them: "I want to hear what you have to say," which also means, "What you have to say is important to me." This implicit message alone validates to your grandchildren that their needs are significant; that they matter.

Grandchildren who have a history of trauma, abuse, neglect, or loss cannot hear too often how important they are to you. Should you tell your grandkids how much you love them? Definitely. Your loving connection with them is what helps them heal and learn to trust again. Your listening and undivided attention says, "I am interested." Should you tell them how fortunate the world is that they are here and how they make the world a better place? Absolutely. In fact, you cannot tell them this too often. As long as the messages you communicate to them are genuine and from your heart, you can never tell your grandchildren too many times how much you love them and how grateful you are to have them in your daily life.

It is important to remember that your using this approach today counters the old, destructive messages that they used to receive, such as: "I don't want you"; or, "If it weren't for you, I would not be in this mess! I could do whatever I want, and I would have enough money to live." And, perhaps the worst message of all: "If I knew then what I know today, I would have never had you!" These messages can be communicated verbally and nonverbally, but, either way, they are extremely hurtful and leave deep wounds.

Keep in mind that children often perceive and understand abandonment, rejection, and neglect on a nonverbal or behavioral level. This can make it even more difficult for them to process and deal with their feelings. The reason for this is most of them learned *not* to express vulnerability to their parents, so "acting out" or "acting in" became the only response they knew.

The most important part of the message that "use your words" conveys to your grandchildren is that you are giving them the voice that they were denied by their parents because of abuse, neglect or loss. By giving them permission to express their needs with language rather than behavior, you empower your grandchildren to stand up for themselves in an appropriate and effective way—and, when they do, they are stronger for it.

A fine program that you might want to look into is the ALERT Program: How Does Your Engine Run? (http://www.alertprogram.com). One of the greatest strengths of this program is that it gives children specific tools to help them understand what they need to learn and how to self-regulate—both of which are powerful skills for any children who have previously resorted to aggression, dissolved into tears, or withdrawn, all in an attempt to get adults to meet their needs.

To sum up, by encouraging them to use their words, you give your grandchildren their voice back. This automatically gives them appropriate levels of control that empower them and help them to begin the healing process from any past trauma that they might have experienced. Giving children a voice is an effective way to prevent behavioral meltdowns ("acting out"), or the opposite response of withdrawal and avoidance ("acting in").

This next story demonstrates the importance of using their words, and it also offers a very effective coping strategy.

> *Anisha is a twelve-year-old girl who spent three years in foster care, after her parents abandoned her when she was five. She now lives with her paternal grandmother, Collette, who has full guardianship of Anisha. During the four years that she has lived with Collette, Anisha has received child therapy and play therapy. Collette joined a grandparent support group through the family-and-child service agency where Anisha receives ongoing treatment.*

When eight-year-old Anisha came to live with Collette, she could not concentrate or sit still. Anisha was also prone to frequent temper tantrums. She seemed inattentive and aloof, and her fears emerged as night time approached. With the help of Anisha's therapist, Collette began to recognize Anisha's behavioral warnings, which indicated that she was about to have a meltdown. Collette would urge Anisha to use language, instead of behavior, to communicate her feelings. "Use your words!" Collette would tell Anisha.

Initially, Anisha was so overcome with emotion that she would freeze. A "freeze" occurs when your mind cannot sort out thoughts sufficiently to allow you to respond to an overwhelming situation. With the help of her therapist, Anisha eventually was able to identify her feelings of frustration and anger. As she became more trusting, she was able to talk about her anxiety.

Collette related a recent event, when one of her own friends was visiting with her, and Anisha interrupted their conversation, asking for some help with her homework. Her grandmother immediately responded to Anisha, telling her granddaughter, "I'll be able to help you in about a half-hour." Anisha replied, "I can't wait anymore, Grandma! I am starting to feel frustrated inside. Please help me now."

Collette realized that she and her friend were still visiting in what was now Anisha's homework time, a time that both grandmother and granddaughter had worked hard to make predictable and repetitive. "This is your homework time, and I'm sorry I'm still visiting with my friend. I'll end the visit now, and you and I will start your homework shortly," Collette told Anisha, so that she could help her granddaughter during their designated time.

This was an important decision for Collette, as Anisha had used her words to express what she was feeling inside. Also, Anisha expected and anticipated the attention and help she had grown accustomed to receiving during her designated homework time—and, significantly, that she and Collette had agreed upon and worked to create.

At this point in her healing, it would not be realistic for Collette to expect Anisha to be able to be flexible about her designated time, so Anisha's reaction was actually typical, as well as indicative of progress. Anisha showed that she feels safe enough to ask for what she needs, and Collette's response acknowledged both those needs and Anisha's progress in managing her feelings and behaviors. Furthermore, Collette's response communicated trust to Anisha, with an implicit message that said, "I hear you, Anisha. I understand your needs, and I am responding to them." Only by establishing trust can Collette expect Anisha to learn and use healthier, more adaptive behaviors.

It is significant to understand that asking for help and feeling heard were big steps not just for Anisha, but also for Collette. Adults don't always like to be interrupted by children, so the responses were a testimony to both granddaughter and grandmother that they had built a safe foundation of communication, whereby Anisha could name her feelings—using words instead of behaviors—and trust that her grandmother would hear and understand her, and then respond to her needs.

In the old days, children who did this to their parents, grandparents, or just about any adult, received a vastly different response, such as: "Wait until the grown-ups are finished talking"; "Don't interrupt!"; or "Don't be rude!" For children raised in stable, loving environments where parents have set this behavior as a "house rule," conveying these messages in a way that firmly but caringly reinforces this rule is appropriate—such as, "I'm talking with my friend right now, but I'll come help you in ten minutes. Please be patient like we've talked about."

But Anisha is a child with a history of abandonment and emotional abuse, and the messages children received in the past would only serve to trigger Anisha's trauma and, significantly, it could damage the trust that grandmother and granddaughter have worked so hard to build.

Both Anisha and Collette made a conscious choice to shift from their old behaviors—to not give in to strong impulses or old ways of being—and, instead, to communicate in ways that expressed a clear need (Anisha) and a clear understanding of that need (Collette).

This is how we build trust, and it is also how we reinforce that the environment in which we raise our grandchildren is safe and predictable. As old patterns give way to new patterns, old ways of behaving give way to new ways of behaving, and old ways of responding give way to new ways of responding; as a result of all this, both you and your grandchildren build confidence in your mutual loving relationship. You must be aware that it will not be a clear, forward path; your grandchildren will move forward and backward, and so will you; they will regress and make mistakes, and so will you—especially when you or they are tired and/or overwhelmed. Thus, it is the *attitude* of commitment to a new way of being in relationship that matters here— and your grandchildren sense that as much as you do!

Storytelling, performing plays, and putting on puppet shows (you can use socks as hand puppets) are just a few of the ways we can help our grandchildren practice and learn to "speak out" (participate in an ongoing conversation), and then "speak up" (represent their point of view and/or defend their own idea or opinion).An alternative is to help children make their own "feeling wheel." Draw a big circle on a good-sized piece of paper, and then draw lines from the center of the circle to the outer edge, in the same way as you would divide a pie. Put three or four words in each slice, and then ask the children to finish the sentence by verbalizing the emotions that they either feel currently, or that they have felt recently, related to a given event.

The feeling wheel is especially useful for children (and adults) who have trouble expressing their emotions. Some individuals feel vulnerable expressing their feelings, and this technique turns it into more of a "game" that everyone participates in—grandchildren and grandparents, as well as close relatives and friends, if your grandchildren feel comfortable including others. This activity makes it even safer to express feelings because everyone can have one "pass" if something is too overwhelming. However, because everyone only gets that one pass, each person needs to think about when—and even if—he or she wants to use it.

In order to use the feeling wheel effectively, schedule it for a specific time each week, and make sure that you keep interruptions to a minimum (shut off the TV and cell phones, do not allow anyone to use their MP3 players or play music, etc.). You and your grandchildren can set your own additional rules, but everyone needs to honor those rules and follow them consistently.

When using the feeling wheel, it is essential that no one interrupt the individual speaking. Everyone gets a turn to share, and no one can comment on what any other person has said except to say something neutral, such as: "Thank you for sharing your feelings"; or, "I heard what you said." This makes each person feel safe, because everyone knows that no judgment or critical feedback follow the sharing of feelings. It also teaches family members how to express emotions in positive, nonjudgmental ways. This communication tool is a very important one for both children and adults, especially those with a history of abuse, neglect, abandonment, or any kind of trauma.

Some examples of what the "prompt statements" in the slices of the feeling wheel might contain include:

- I get scared when _____.

- It hurts my feelings when _____.

- I am happy when _____.

- I laugh when _____.

- I cry when _____.

- I get nervous when _____.

- I feel embarrassed when _____.

- I feel frustrated when _____.

- I want to thank you for _____.

- I get angry when _____.

- I feel confused when _____.

- I love _____.

- I need you to understand me when I _____.

- I feel safer when _____.

- I wish you _____.

Here is an example of a Feeling Wheel. Your grandchildren can circle the wheel completing each statement; or they can limit their comments to specific statements.

Feeling Wheel

I am proud of myself when I…

I feel safer when I…

I am happy when…

I get scared when…

I feel frustrated when I…

I get jealous when…

I get angry when…

I feel embarrassed when I…

For younger children (eight years old or less) and/or for children with verbal challenges, you can use colors, instead of words, to help them describe their feelings. If using colors, everyone needs to agree what each color represents. For instance, blue might mean feeling okay, I can manage things; red might denote "hot" emotions like anger, impatience, and frustration; green can indicate jealousy or envy; yellow might represent joy, cheerfulness and happiness; orange might mean being pleased or proud of oneself.; black might denote sadness or unhappiness; brown might show a dislike for something or someone; and white might represent feeling confused, uncertain or nervous.

Here is an example of a feeling wheel that uses colors instead of words:

Color Wheel

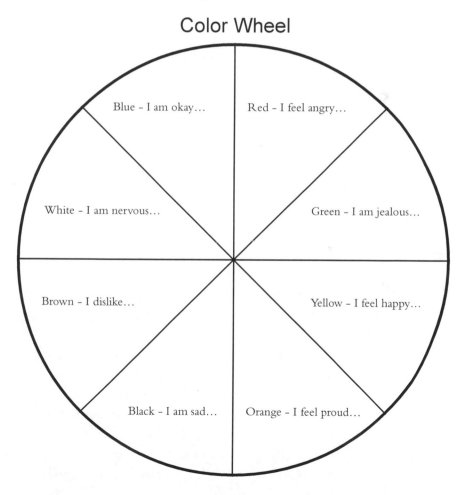

This is how I felt this past week.

- When I tried to do my homework by myself, I felt like the color **red.**

- When the other kids were teasing me, I felt like the color **brown.**

- When I scored a goal in my soccer game, I felt like the color **yellow.**

- When my mom did not show up, even though she promised to, I felt like the color **black.**

- When you baked some cupcakes for me to take to school, I felt like the color **orange.**

- Even though some of the kids in my class said you were old, I felt like the color **blue.**

- When you pay more attention to my brother than to me, it makes me feel like the color **green.**

You can change the "prompt statements" from time to time, or you can leave them the same each time you and your grandchildren use it—whether you use a regular feeling wheel, the color version, or both. Be sure to include some of your grandchildren's suggestions as to what should appear on the feeling wheel.

Using the feeling wheel will help your grandchildren express and share their emotions in a safe and unique way. It also invests them in a positive process that teaches and reinforces constructive ways to express feelings. Over time, the feeling wheel can become a practical tool for the entire family to use in order to develop and maintain good, safe communication skills. It also teaches us to be more aware of our own feelings, as well as those of others. Ultimately—and perhaps most important of all—the feeling wheel may become a replacement for "acting out" or "acting in."

You can also use a tape recorder or a cell phone recorder when your grandchildren are talking about their feelings. Children love to hear the sound of their voice, and listening to themselves speak is another way of reinforcing the power of words in an appropriate way. Plus, because so many of your grandchildren have never received the permission or invitation to speak, giving voice to their feelings and thoughts is a wonderful way to validate them.

You and your grandchildren can end the feeling wheel activity with some quiet reflective time, alone or together. Whatever you decide is the appropriate closing for this weekly activity, it is vital for you and your grandkids to view this time as sacred, predictable, and important. Respecting each other's responses needs to be a consistent expectation held by all participants. This activity should not continue any longer than the youngest participant can handle. Ideally, it should last for at least fifteen minutes and not more than forty-five minutes, depending on the number of participants.

Create a Safe, Predictable, and Desirable Environment

One of the most dynamic tools for helping your at-risk grandchildren is to create an environment in which they know that they are safe. This does not imply that the children are not safe now with you; rather, what it means is that your grandchildren *may need to be reminded* that they are safe. Children who feel safe are free from anxiety, worry, and obsessive thinking (i.e., about whether the doors are locked, the shades are drawn, etc.) For the most part, you can create this feeling of security by making the children's world predictable, and, as stated previously, by giving them appropriate levels of control so that they do not lapse into old behaviors of "acting out" or "acting in." When you create a safe environment by making their world predictable and giving them appropriate levels of control, you will give your grandchildren the optimal opportunity to develop and grow.

For example, establishing before- and after-school routines that are repetitive—and, therefore, predictable—communicates key messages to your grandchildren, including what you expect from them, how to organize their time, and also how to balance necessary tasks and activities (work, school, family time, etc.). You can use these routines to teach them decision-making skills, too. By allowing them to choose between playing outside for an hour before doing homework, or doing homework first and then playing outside for an hour, you offer them the opportunity to participate in the choice and feel empowered, but in a way that gives them appropriate control.

Other environmental considerations are important, as well. Look at your grandchildren's bedroom, in particular. Whether they each have their own room or share with a sibling, the room should be a soothing color and the children should choose the color, if possible. Again, this gives them the power of choice, along with appropriate control about how their room will look and feel. The price of a gallon of paint is worth the sense of importance and respect your grandchildren will experience, as well as the validation they will feel afterward.

In general, soothing colors are those that we can find in nature, and that relax the mind, body, and spirit. Different shades of green and blue, gold and tans, and the softer shades of pink and lavender, all are examples of soothing colors. More vivid colors—reds, purples, and all the "neon" shades of any color—may appeal to your grandchildren, but are not soothing for rooms where teens and children rest and sleep! If you cannot abide certain colors, let your grandchildren know what is off-limits and what is acceptable. For instance, you could say, "I know that purple is your favorite color, but 'fluorescent grape' is going to make it hard for you to fall asleep. How about choosing one of these softer lilacs or lavenders instead?" Let them accompany you to the paint store to collect samples that they can bring home and compare. Again, all this empowers their choices but in a way that allows only appropriate levels of control.

After painting the room, sit down with each grandchild and decide together what they will put back into the room, and what they will leave out. Ask your grandchildren what they would like to keep in their room that will help them feel safe and secure while they spend time in their room playing, studying, sleeping, etc. If they have a hard time parting with some objects, but these objects do not pass the "safe and secure" test, place them elsewhere in your home.

Some children and teens have pictures of dinosaurs, monsters, or superheroes in their bedroom. They may love these images, however, these pictures can look foreboding in nighttime darkness, and they might actually scare your grandchildren—even if they refuse to admit that. Religious images or symbols in their room may make them feel fearful, too.

To pass the "safe and secure" test, images or objects have to support children's and teens' confidence and comfort in being alone in their own rooms. These images and objects must not stir feelings of fear or tension, either during the day or at night. Again, some children may be reluctant to tell you that something on the wall is scary, so use that wonderful "sixth sense" you have as a grandparent. Often, simply asking them will give you your answer.

This story illustrates the importance of creating a soothing bedroom environment for your grandchildren.

> *Thad is an eleven-year-old twin who has many fears and anxieties. He lived in an orphanage until he was adopted at the age of five. Thad's adoptive parents provided a safe and loving home, but when Thad was eight, his father was killed in an auto accident, which forced his mother to look for full-time work. Thad lives with his maternal grandparents during the week, and he spends the weekends with his mother.*
>
> *When he moved in with his grandparents, Emily and William, Thad's bedroom was a wine color, and it was located in the back of the upper level, quite separate from the other bedrooms on the same floor. Thad disliked sleeping in his bedroom; so much so that, invariably, one of his grandparents ended up sleeping with him at*

some point during the night. Thad also complained of seeing faces in the windows during the night, which scared him and caused him to have bad dreams.

When interviewed, Thad's grandparents, expressed that they were both concerned and perplexed by Thad's fears, as they believed that they had made a good, safe home for Thad during the week. From their perspective they had, but they needed to realize that Thad needed to define and express his own feelings of safety. Thad's grandparents were willing to listen to what he believed would make him less fearful.

Thad wanted his bedroom to be a different color. He wished his grandparents would paint it 'celery green'. Thad was very specific about the color, and, although his grandparents did not understand why that shade of green was so important to Thad, they acknowledged his feelings and honored his request. Thad and William went to several hardware stores before they found the exact color Thad wanted. Both grandson and grandparents were quite pleased with the outcome.

After repainting, Thad's room was considerably brighter and more pleasant to be in. Following some additional discussion with Thad, William removed some pictures and objects that had caused Thad anxiety, and he replaced them with a few objects—a picture of an eagle soaring above a valley and a small statuette of a horse, both of which appealed to Thad and which he felt comfortable having in his bedroom.

In the meantime, Emily, made some window curtains to keep out the shadows of the night. The curtains were plain and simple, which added to the growing brightness of the room. While it took a couple of years for Thad to be able to sleep alone, it did not take long at all for him to go into his bedroom alone to play, read, and study.

This was a very simple, yet very effective, solution. Thad felt very special because his grandparents involved him in the process of making his room safer and more pleasant. His self-confidence grew, and Thad even began to bring a couple of neighborhood friends over to play in his room.

Your grandchildren's bedroom needs to be a sanctuary for supporting their internal security. That does not necessarily mean purchasing new furniture or anything particularly expensive; however, it does mean being very selective about what is in the room, all of which must support the safety of your grandchildren's emotional life.

De-cluttering is also important. Not only does it allow for fewer distractions, it also creates fewer triggers and provides less assault on the senses. In addition, fewer objects in the room will create fewer shadows, which sometimes can trigger fears, especially at night. Some children are afraid of leaving their windows open or their shades up, nervous that some "creature" will look in the window or even climb into the room through the open window. This may just be their active imaginations, but to them it could be "real," so prevent unnecessary fear by having a discussion with them about what you can do to make them feel safer.

One grandmother bought a plain, inexpensive window shade. She and her granddaughter, Ashley, decorated the room-facing side of the shade together so that it met the "safe and secure" test. They drew a big sun on the bottom of the shade and a half moon at the top. At night, when they pulled the shade all the way down, Ashley could see the moon—"her moon," as she liked to call it. In the morning, when they raised the shade, the big sun that Ashley had drawn smiled at her. They also placed glow-in-the-dark stickers and stars on the ceiling, which Ashley loved to look at as she drifted off to sleep. With so much of her own artwork as part of the decoration of her room, Ashley not only felt proud of what she had done to her room, but she also felt considerably less fearful about her window, as the shadows were now gone.

Once you've seen to your grandchildren's bedroom, consider walking through the rest of your home with your grandchildren to see if any of the other rooms either soften or exaggerate the children's fears. Basements are notorious for stimulating children's fears and imaginations. More basements have held imaginary monsters, ghosts, strange noises, and scary shadows than other parts of homes. Go down to the basement together, and allow your grandchildren to become de-sensitized to all the sounds, shadows, and other potentially scary things.

Attics, closets, and cellars are other parts of the house that may foster fearful or anxious feelings. You may want to ask your grandchild if particular areas of the basement—attic, cellar, closet, or any other room—are bothersome or "scary." Additional lighting can help with shadows; plus, removing objects that you no longer need, and that only add to clutter, can help make the basement feel more comfortable for your grandchildren—and for you.

Think carefully when you initiate creating a safe, secure home environment. Some grandparents may inadvertently make their grandchildren feel self-conscious or embarrassed by saying things that sound critical or judgmental about their fears, such as "You're too big to be afraid to go to bed by yourself"; "You are eleven now. It's time you stopped being such a scaredy-cat"; "You are just a big sissy!", and so on. Remember the importance of moving away from push-and-pull patterns; you certainly don't want to create new ones. (Refer back to chapter 6.)

Statements like these, aside from hurting your grandchildren's feelings, also trigger old messages of rejection—of being a bother, of not being good enough, or of thinking that something is wrong with them. In addition, many grandchildren may be a certain chronological age, but, because of their traumas, developmentally, they may be far younger—that is, stuck in a younger developmental life stage, as discussed in chapter 4. The one message your grandchildren need to receive consistently from you is that you understand their fears, love them unconditionally, and will keep them safe and secure.

Grandparents of the Silent Generation (that is, those born before 1945) may feel like this is too much accommodation. If you are of this generation, you may feel like you are spoiling your grandkids, or giving in to them too much. If these thoughts or beliefs arise for you, remind yourself how much more we know about children's and teen's developmental challenges now than we did when we ourselves were children and when we were parenting our own kids. This additional information gives us a deeper understanding of our children and their needs—especially those who have a history of trauma, abuse, neglect, or loss.

Daily Schedules and Activities

Let *predictability* be the mantra in your home, and the guiding principle of the schedules that you and your grandchildren create. Build enough time into morning routines, in particular, as many children take a long time to get going in the morning. However, daily daytime routines may also offer challenges because of uncooperative behaviors often referred to as *resistance*. Examples of resistance include moving slowly, refusing to get out of bed, not paying attention, crying or whining, complaints of "I can't____!", and so on. Other interferences include unexpected occurrences, such as the telephone or doorbell ringing, a missing shoe, one or more of the grandkids not feeling well, experiencing multiple demands from multiple grandchildren simultaneously, and so on. Notice that resistance actually can, and will, occur at any time of the day or night!

In the case of a single grandparent and two or more grandchildren, try to stagger wake-up times, even if the children all leave for school at the same time. A staggered schedule will make it easier for you to guide them and give some individualized attention to those who need it. You may want to wake your slowest-moving grandchild first, and then begin the morning with him or her. When that child realizes that, by getting ready more quickly, he or she could sleep longer, it provides a good incentive to speed up!

If both grandparents are present in the home, you can divide the responsibility for getting your grandchildren up and going between the two of you. After school, you can divide it again, except that each grandparent takes the opposite grandchild from the morning, so that each child has some one-on-one time with each grandparent. This approach may also derail any accusations by your grandchildren of having or playing favorites.

These are just options. The final decision is yours, because you know what works best for each child. Some grandfathers find it easier to work with their grandsons or older grandkids. However, preferences are very individualized, as many grandfathers are actually better at braiding their granddaughter's hair than their grandmothers are! What is most important is discussing your morning, after-school, and evening routines together as a family.

As much as possible, you need to keep established schedules and routines for your grandchildren. When each of your grandchildren has experienced success mastering a schedule, it builds self-confidence and sense of competence. One of the most important things you do for your grandchildren when you make their daily routines predictable is that you give them the experience of being in control of their lives—of being more independent and competent. Being able to anticipate expectations allows your grandchildren the best opportunity to experience success, which is the ultimate goal.

If schedules must change, which is certainly bound to happen, grandchildren need as much notice as possible in order to internally adjust to the changes. Children who come from trauma do not handle sudden change easily. The suddenness of a change, no matter how insignificant it might seem to you, is often a major trigger to the past— parents' tempers flaring; erratic shifts in parents' moods; eruptions of parents' arguments, yelling, or even violence; and so on—in any event, the most minor change can instantaneously hurl your grandchildren inwardly back to that prior time when they felt helpless, out of control, unsafe, and possibly victimized. It bears repeating that keeping things predictable provides your grandchildren with a new foundation upon which they can build trust, confidence, and a sense of competence.

Working Agreements

One of the best ways to ensure that your grandchildren will invest in daily routines is to have them be an important part of the planning of those routines. It is vitally important to have family discussions about the needs and expectations of grandparents and grandchildren. This approach will go a long way in reducing resistance by your grandchildren. If your grandchildren are too young to participate in this kind of discussion, it is important to spend some quiet time together, during which you explain your decisions to them. As soon as they are old enough to understand and contribute their thoughts and ideas to the conversation, you should include younger children in these discussions.

Working agreements should be written on a chart and placed on a wall where it is a daily reminder of the family members' commitments to each other. Ask the question: What will it take for all of us to be the best family we can be? Every member of the family should offer at least one response, so everyone is represented. At least once a week, the family should come together to discuss how well the Working Agreements are working. This is also a good time to decide if anything needs to be added, deleted or made more clear.

My thirteen-year-old granddaughter is very clear about her need for quiet time. We don't always think of teenagers as needing or wanting quiet time, but they do. Whether it is viewed as quiet time or private time be sure to give your grandkids permission to ask for what they need. Once they learn that you hear and understand their needs, they will begin to verbalize them eliminating any guess work on your part. Asking for what you need is a great item to add to your working agreements. If no one mentions it, ask if it is okay to add it to the family's list of working agreements.

"Working agreements" are just what they imply: ongoing agreements by every member of the family to behave according to the guidelines and agreed-upon arrangements that everyone has participated in creating, and that everyone is willing to make a commitment to keeping. These agreements are not just made *to* or *for* grandparents. Every individual member of the family has an obligation to every other member of the family to keep their promise to honor the working agreements. In essence, it is a family effort; in the business world, it is known as *teamwork*.

High-performing teams do four things, in particular, that make them successful: (1) each team member commits to a common purpose, and to shared goals and values; (2) each team member commits to good, open communication (also called "conversation"); (3) each team member understands and respects the common intention and meaning of the conversation; and (4) each member buys into the shared vision and common values of the team.

Your grandchildren might be a little young to understand some of these ideas; however, regardless of age, children learn to communicate verbally and nonverbally based on how authentic the adults in their lives are—that is, how much the children trust the adults in their lives, and how safe it is for them to be truthful. In essence, strong functioning families—like high-performing teams—are able to live their values and beliefs, communicate honestly and respectfully, feel safe to be their genuine selves, and trust that each family member is important and matters to the whole family.

Self-Reflection Questions for Parenting Grandparents

Here are some questions to ask yourselves as parenting grandparents. The answers to these questions will tell you if yours is a strong functioning family—the more yes answers, the stronger your family unit is likely to be.

- Do your grandchildren trust you? Can you think of some examples in which they show their trust in you?

- Can you hear your grandchildren's truth without getting angry or judgmental? Be aware that your ability to hear them, without anger or judgment, will reduce their lying to you.

- Does your home environment support physical and emotional safety and security for each family member?

- Are you and your grandchildren authentic when you communicate with each other? In other words, are your words, thoughts, behaviors, and emotions in alignment, or do they change if any one of you senses disapproval?

- Are you able to have difficult conversations in respectful and honest ways?

- Are you a good listener? Can you listen to your grandchildren without framing any thoughts in your head as they are talking? Are you teaching your grandchildren to be good listeners?

- Do you talk about family values and beliefs? Does each family member display behaviors that complement the family's values and beliefs?

- Do you stop what you are doing and take time to listen to your grandchildren when they are upset? Do you encourage them to "use their words" instead of "acting out" or "acting in" their emotions?

- Does each family member understand their responsibilities? Does everyone do his or her assigned tasks Does everyone understand how interdependent their responsibilities and tasks are?

- Do you help your grandchildren own their problems and challenges? Do you help them find and use their own age-appropriate solutions?

This next story illustrates the importance of communication and mutual commitment to creating and honoring family agreements.

Twelve-year-old Alec has lived with his grandmother, Sharon, for seven years. Over the last year, Sharon has noticed Alec coming home later and later for dinner, and then skipping his evening chores because he claims to have too much homework. Sharon admits to nagging Alec about both his tardiness and his not being responsible for his evening chores. As time passes, nothing changes, and both Sharon and Alec have become moody and bicker more frequently.

When Alec and Sharon came to see me, it was immediately evident how much they cared about each other. This was a good place to begin. After mentioning how I could see that they loved each other very much, I wondered out loud why they behaved in ways that each knew would upset the other.

Alec felt picked on, and Sharon felt taken advantage of. Once they both understood how their words and behaviors were negatively affecting each other, I again wondered aloud if they could figure out a solution that would be acceptable to both of them.

I helped them both verbalize what they needed from each other. Sharon needed for Alec to be home in time for dinner and to complete his evening chores and homework. Alec needed his grandmother to stop nagging him and being out of sorts.

When I asked Alec what he thought it would take for him to be home in time for dinner so he could get all his work done, he told me he wished dinner could be a little later. Alec said if dinner were later, he would be eating the same time his friends were eating, and then he would be home on time for sure! I encouraged Alec to discuss this with his grandmother, which he did. Her concern was that he would have even less time after dinner to do everything that he needed to do.

Alec really wanted a later dinner, which offered his grandmother an opportunity to ask if he could get his homework done before he went to hang out with his friends. Alec said that, if dinner were later, he would work harder during his study hall at school in order to get more of his homework done. He promised that he would complete any unfinished homework as soon as he came home from school. Sharon thought this was a great solution, and, even better it was her grandson's solution. She agreed to make dinner one hour later to coordinate with Alec's friends' dinnertime. Not only did Alec resume doing his chores when dinner was over, he and Sharon had time to play a game or watch a little TV together before bedtime.

Both you, as parenting grandparents, and your grandchildren have to bend a little, as you all are learning the skills of problem-solving, negotiation, and compromise.

Exercise and Nutrition

Exercise is an important healing activity for children who have a history of abuse, neglect, abandonment, and/or other trauma. If your grandchildren do not participate in sports, it is especially important that they engage in physical exercise on a daily basis. Suitable levels of exercise can release the feel-good hormones in the brain, especially serotonin, which is elevated through activities that consist of repetitive movements sustained for a reasonable period of time.

These activities might include bike riding, jumping rope, playing ball, jogging, yoga, skateboarding, dancing, swimming, etc. Activities like these are inexpensive, and your grandchildren can do them at home or at a community playground, as well as in school gyms. Exercise also reduces stress hormones, such as cortisol and/or adrenaline, and this reduction will help prevent adrenal fatigue. Also, if your grandchildren are prediabetic, exercise is an excellent way to manage blood sugar. (Be sure that the pediatrician or family doctor approves the exercise regimen.)

Your expectation that your grandchildren will engage in daily exercise activities should be as strong as your expectation that they will complete their homework and household chores. Exercise is a great life tool and an excellent daily habit to develop early in life. The earlier they develop this positive habit, the more likely it will be that your grandchildren continue to exercise on a daily basis, as they will realize the physical and emotional benefits of doing so.

Exercise is also important for grandparents. We need age-appropriate exercise in order to maintain our own health and well-being as much as our grandchildren need it in order to maintain theirs. In fact, grandparents and grandchildren exercising together offers another bonding opportunity where you can support each other's commitment to better physical, mental, and emotional health and wellness.

There are some DVDs of simple Yoga, Tai Chi, and Pilates that stretch muscles gently, and have a relaxing effect on the body, mind, and spirit. You and your grandchildren can do the exercises on these videos together. (I use Kim Eng's "Qi Flow Yoga." Remember, for yourselves and your grandchildren, be sure to consult a physician prior to embarking on any exercise regimen.)

A nutritious diet is also very important for health and well-being. Diets high in fiber and vegetables—unless otherwise indicated by your or your grandchildren's physician—are ideal. While fresh vegetables can be expensive, here are a few tips from some of the parenting grandparents interviewed:

1. The most important decision you can make about your grandchildren's nutrition is to eliminate, or at least limit, foods high in sugar, such as candy, gum, soda pop, cookies, cake, pie, etc. These foods consist of empty calories, and, even worse, they make blood sugar rise and fall. This means your grandchildren's behaviors and moods may be erratic; they can quickly go from being overly active or inattentive to tired and sluggish.

2. Be careful to read the active ingredients in the foods you purchase in order to determine if they contain high-fructose corn syrup. This is a controversial sugar found in foods that we don't ordinarily think would have a high sugar content, such as ketchup, cereals, breakfast bars, etc.

3. Moderation is key, but knowing which foods have a high sugar content is important in managing your grandchildren's nutrition.

4. Carbohydrates are tricky also, as many of them convert into sugar. It is important to know the difference between simple and complex carbohydrates.

   Generally, simple carbohydrates are any food that contains sugar, including:

   • white table sugar

   • honey

   • candy

   • regular soda pop

   • many processed snack foods

   • molasses

   • milk and some dairy products

   • ice cream and frozen yogurt

   • sherbet and ices

   • jams and jellies

All the above foods contain one or more of the various forms of sugar (sucrose, fructose, maltose, dextrose, glucose, etc.; the "-ose" ending means it's a sugar). As a result, these foods are absorbed into the bloodstream very quickly, causing a spike in insulin levels and an increase in fat storage (among other negative health effects); after the blood-sugar levels spike, they plummet.

With the exception of fruits and low-fat dairy products (low-fat or nonfat milk, yogurt, cottage cheese, and other low-fat or nonfat cheeses), simple carbohydrates should be avoided—especially when trying to lose body fat and improve overall health.

Complex carbohydrates are generally healthier than simple carbohydrates. They take much longer to digest; often, but not always, they contain a good amount of vitamins, minerals, and fiber. Examples of complex carbohydrates include:

- vegetables

- legumes

- oatmeal

- whole-grain cereals

- whole-grain breads

- whole-grain pasta

By far, the best (i.e., healthiest) complex carbohydrates are vegetables and legumes (beans, peas, etc.). Usually, when people speak of "good carbohydrates," those are what they're referring to. The next-best form of complex carbohydrates are oatmeal, and any whole-grain breads, cereals, and pastas. These provide ample fiber, and it's ideal to consume them in small amounts several times a day. Whole-grain breads and dry whole-grain cereals or cereal bars also offer great snack options for kids and teens.

Finally, breads, pastas, and cereals made from refined white flour are the worst type of complex carbohydrates to eat. Don't be fooled by the labeling that says they are "enriched"! These foods cause many of the same negative effects in the body as simple carbohydrates because they quickly convert to sugar. For the most part, you should avoid, or at least limit, these carbohydrates.

The above lists show just a few examples of simple complex carbohydrates, intended to give you a good idea of how to establish a nutritious diet for you and your grandchildren. You can find more information at www.fitFAQ.com.

Remember, for yourselves and your grandchildren, be sure to consult a physician prior to embarking on any diet or nutrition regimen.

5. Good nutrition is key, but eating healthfully can strain food budgets. Know when and where to shop for sales and specials. For instance, local farmers' markets are great places to find fresh food at reasonable prices—and support farmers in your community. Plus, if you shop thirty minutes before they close, you often can negotiate the price of your purchase, as they would rather sell the product that day than have to pack it up.

   Check the newspapers and note the times of the month when meat, dairy, produce, and other nutritious items are on sale in the supermarket or local stores. In many places, these are not on sale at the same time, so you may have to shop a bit more often and in different stores in order to take advantage of the sales and specials.

   Some food warehouses have good discounts for bulk purchases. So, if your family is large, or if you have a good-sized freezer, Costco, Sam's Club or Meijer might be good places for you to shop. In addition, ask members of grandparent support groups if they would like to shop in bulk and then divide the food and the cost.

Perhaps the best suggestion of all is from one grandfather who planted a garden with the help of his two granddaughters, ages ten and eight. Cultivating the produce that they were able to enjoy as part of healthy, nutritious meals was a terrific experience for the entire family, as well as being an inexpensive way to increase consumption of veggies.

Finally, your teen grandchildren—both boys and girls—can learn to cook. Soups and stews are easy to learn how to prepare, and they are nutritious "comfort foods." This is also another opportunity for some shared family time; it can be very helpful and productive, while also teaching a life skill. All too quickly, teens are ready to go out on their own—either to pursue higher education or enter the working world—and knowing how to prepare nutritious meals inexpensively is a skill they will use for the rest of their lives.

Tips for Managing Grandchildren with ADHD or ADD

If your grandchild has Attention Deficit Hyperactivity Disorder (ADHD) or Attention Deficit Disorder (ADD), consider some important things that you can do to support his or her success at school and at home (*see* list that follows this paragraph). This list is applicable to children who have Asperger's Syndrome, Dyslexia and other conditions that influence their concentration and behaviors in social settings. Teachers frequently suggest an Individualized Education Plan (IEP) for children with ADHD or ADD. Please be sure to discuss an IEP with the school principal, school counselor, and your grandchild's teacher.

- **Communicate with the teacher.** Communication between you, your grandchild, and the teacher should be clear and frequent. A weekly conversation is the minimal standard, but more frequent communication is desirable. Be sure to discuss your grandchild's behavior both at school and at home.

To complement any plan implemented by the school, parenting grandparents need to develop an Individualized Home Plan (IHP). This will ensure consistency, predictability, and successful experiences for your grandchild. Here are some tips that should prove especially helpful. Many of these tips came from Parenting.com, a website highly recommended for all parenting grandparents.

- **Be consistent.** Establish a daily routine, beginning at morning wake-up time, continuing through dinnertime, and ending with bedtime. Snacks, homework, dinnertime, playtime, and bedtime should be as close to the same time as possible every day. This establishes important habits and patterns, which gives your grandchild considerable predictability.

- **Stay on schedule.** Post schedules around the house outlining what happens every day during the hours before and after school. This will help keep everyone on track—not just the grandchild with ADHD/ADD.

- **Calm the environment.** As your grandchildren prepare to do their homework or chores, make sure the house is quiet and distractions are limited. Make this slow-time---doing so encourages focus and concentration. You may want to pull down the shades or draw the drapes as a signal for quiet time.

- **Calm your grandchildren.** Some children have a hard time slowing down from a busy day. Have your grandkids do some deep breathing, individually or together. Perhaps, they can lie down for a few minutes just to let their mind and body know a shift is occurring. Make this time a quiet period.

- **Establish homework time.** Specify a time for doing and completing homework. Some children need to come home and relax a little bit, while others do better getting their homework done first and then having free time. Discuss these options with your grandchildren, and then you can decide whether each grandchild needs his or her own schedule, or if they all will do their homework at the same time. Be available during homework time to answer questions and offer support. Frequent positive feedback about how each child is doing encourages your grandchildren and also keeps them focused.

- **Eliminate distractions.** Switching off the TV set, cell phones, iPods, etc. at homework time is a must. TV and video games should be off-limits for everyone when your grandchildren are doing homework. Just knowing that someone else is getting screen or game time is a distraction for children with ADHD/ADD. You also can designate specified "quiet time" regardless of whether your grandchildren have homework. Learning to take time to read, relax, or just otherwise be silent is an important experience for children to have, even those without ADHD/ADD.

- **Limit "screen time."** TV and video games can really over stimulate and distract children with ADHD/ADD. You need to create a positive reward system for your grandchildren when they finish homework and chores.

This might mean less TV time for everyone in the family, but it will allow more time for conversations, games, creativity, exercise, playing, and spending time together as a family.

- **Assign tasks to your grandchildren.** When you have a task or assignment for your ADHD/ADD grandchildren, provide short, clear directions. If you have several tasks, communicate them one at a time, allowing your grandchildren time to repeat these instructions back to you, demonstrating what they heard and understood. This ensures good communication, as well as clear mutual understanding. It also provides a greater likelihood that your grandchildren will successfully complete the assigned task—this, in turn, fosters self-confidence and a sense of accomplishment, important to all children, but especially those with ADHD/ADD.

- **Use a system for assignments.** Visual cues that accompany verbal directions are very helpful to all children, especially those with ADHD/ADD. You can create folders or charts for their assigned tasks, and then you can check them off together every day. Charts and folders are easy to color code by day of the week. For instance, Monday might be blue; Tuesday, green; and so on. Folders or charts should have spaces labeled "to do" and "done." For younger children, use stars or stickers to indicate completed tasks. Find age-appropriate ways to make task completion fun for your grandchildren— both those with and without ADHD/ADD.

- **Organize backpacks.** Help your ADHD/ADD grandchildren empty and sort out their backpacks right after school (i.e., before homework time). Check for notes from the teacher, and weed out unnecessary objects on a daily basis. Help your grandkids repack their backpacks before bed, including any school assignments, gym clothes, library books, notes, etc. ADHD/ADD kids may need assistance even into their teen years, but, as they get older, you can teach them how to manage organizational skills on their own.

- **Break it down.** If your grandchildren feel overwhelmed by any task, break it down into smaller and more manageable steps. For example, the task is to clean his or her bedroom) on Saturday mornings, don't just say, "Clean your bedroom every Saturday morning." Be more specific, saying, "Change the sheets on your bed, dust your nightstand and bookcase, put all your toys in the box, and vacuum your carpet." Smaller goals feel much more reachable, and checking things off the list is gratifying.

- **Limit choices.** For children with ADHD/ADD, having too many choices can be overwhelming. Even fun choices can be hard for these children. Help your grandchild stay on target by limiting their decisions to two or three choices instead of offering too many options.

As parenting grandparents, you may decide to add to, or subtract from, the above list of tips. After all, no one knows your grandchildren better than you do! Just know that working from a list offers both you and your grandchildren predictability and consistency—as well as a greater likelihood of short- and long-term success. Success is the ultimate goal and also the foundation for desired growth.

Gentle Reminders

1. Look for patterns that may trigger your grandchildren's "acting in" or "acting out" behaviors. Triggers can be

anything—words, body language, tone of voice, facial expressions, etc.—that set off, or activate, painful memories or experiences for your grandchildren.

2. When we encourage children to verbalize their needs, we empower them to stand up for themselves, and we also reinforce that their needs are important.

3. A fine program that helps children learn specific tools for understanding what they need and for achieving self-regulation is the "ALERT Program: How Does Your Engine Run?" (http://www.alertprogram.com).

4. Encouraging your grandchildren to discover their own solutions for their problems, fears, and concerns, as well as learning ways to meet their identified needs, really empowers them. It helps them realize that they have inner resources and strengths, and this supports their developing the ability to continue to meet their own needs.

5. Check out parenting.com for more tips on creating routines at home that will give your grandchildren the consistency they need to feel secure and successful.

6. Ask your grandchildren for ideas, suggestions, and solutions when problems and challenges arise. Of course, their ideas should reflect their age and maturity, but children, like adults, will be more invested in activities when they own the ideas. When grandchildren become "solution seekers," they learn important life skills, for the present and the future, and this also makes your parenting work a whole lot easier.

8

HOPE, COURAGE, AND HEALING

The last chapter of this book shares a poignant story that offers hope, not only for your grandchildren, but for their parent(s)—your adult children—and for you. This story reflects core components of so many of the stories in this book, as well as the hundreds of thousands of stories in communities across our country, where grandparents are raising their grandchildren. May this story also inspire you, and offer you courage and healing, as well.

> Maria came to live with her maternal grandparents shortly after she was born in 1986. Her biological mother, Debbie, was seventeen years old at the time. Following Maria's birth, Debbie moved back in with her parents, Rhonda and Daniel. (As a result of Debbie's extremely troubled growing-up years, she had been away at a state-sponsored program. Debbie's own story follows at the end of this chapter.) For two years, Debbie worked two jobs, trying to make ends meet while raising Maria with the help of her parents.
>
> Debbie, a high-school dropout, was addicted to alcohol prior to her pregnancy. During and after her pregnancy, she did not drink. As time passed, however, the stress of working two jobs and being a new, unmarried mom living with her own parents, led Debbie into the drug scene. Her new drug of choice became cocaine.
>
> Feeling overwhelmed, angry, and depressed, Debbie left home and moved to another state, leaving Maria behind. Eventually, Debbie gave custody of eighteen-month-old Maria to Rhonda and Daniel. Over the next twenty years, Debbie called her parents occasionally, but she did not see them or her daughter.

Debbie, an adopted child, is the middle of three sisters. Her older sister, Carol, also adopted, was away at college when their parents obtained custody of Maria, and her younger sister, Jane, was fifteen years old, in high school, and still living at home. As Maria began to walk and talk, she referred to her grandparents as "Mom" and "Dad." She adamantly called her two aunts her "sisters."

It was clear to Rhonda and Daniel, from very early on, that Maria wanted to fit into the family as a daughter and sister, not a granddaughter and niece. When she was old enough to realize that her last name was different from her grandparents', Maria insisted that her surname be changed so that it was the same as rest of the family's. When she was born, her biological father had his last name put on her birth certificate even though he neither married Debbie, nor helped raise Maria.

Even as a young child, Maria was headstrong about being a full-fledged member of the family. She wanted roots, and being a daughter rather than a granddaughter, was her way of obtaining the security she needed at such a tender age.

The internal emptiness children feel when they have been abandoned by their biological and/or adoptive parents is ever present. This leads some children to exhibit aggressive behaviors, which reflect their anger and fury; other children respond by becoming passive and withdrawn; still others, like Maria, become assertive and demanding.

Regardless of the path they choose to express their internal world ("acting out," "acting in," or somewhere in between), all these children feel a painful hole inside. They may well spend their entire lives trying to fill this hole; some are fortunate to succeed, at least to some degree, while others never do. Many of these children have tumultuous teen years, where their "acting out" leads to increasingly destructive behavior—drugs, alcohol, promiscuity, criminal activities, etc. Some engage in blaming behaviors, where they perpetually cast themselves as victims. Others become increasingly placating, trying to please everyone in order to obtain the love they so deeply crave. Still others choose isolation and avoidance. As you can see, the paths these children ultimately choose to follow are quite disparate. However, the one thing that remains the same is that, without your love—and, many times, therapeutic interventions—they become disconnected from their emotions and stuck in a negative life cycle.

Let's go back to the story of Maria and her family.

The transition that the family went through as Maria became a part of their everyday life, was not a natural one. Rhonda and Daniel were both grieving the loss of their daughter, Debbie, whom they were unable to help, regardless of what they tried to do for and with her. It felt awkward to hear little Maria calling them Mama and Daddy, instead of Grandma and Grandpa, which they naturally preferred, as she was their granddaughter.

This is one of the painful transitions very few grandparents talk about when they begin raising their grandchildren. Another painful transition is the overwhelming heartache Rhonda and Daniel felt because Debbie could not get her own life together. They experienced a wide range of emotions from, guilt and anger to sadness and fear. It was also a major shift for Carol and Jane to make when their niece, Maria, entered into the place of their sister, Debbie.

During such transitions, life can feel quite confusing and challenging— it is as if the world has turned upside down, and you are no longer sure of things. It is especially important during this transition phase to have someone you can talk to and confide in—a close friend, a pastor or spiritual advisor, a therapist or counselor—someone you feel safe with, who will understand what you are going through, without judging you or your family.

With three children to support (Carol in college, Jane in high school, and two-year-old Maria), Rhonda and Daniel were strapped, financially.

Besides the financial challenges, parenting grandparents face many other predicaments—both predictable and unpredictable.

Rhonda described the time she took little Maria to the Public Health Department for her immunization shots. This was not where she had taken her own daughters for their immunizations, but she needed to save money, and this seemed like a good option. However, when the nurses realized that Rhonda was Maria's grandmother and not her mother, they denied Maria her shots, as they needed a parent's signature.

Rhonda felt confused and frustrated: She and Daniel were responsible for raising Maria, but, legally, they did not have parental rights. In order for Maria to get her immunizations, they had to ask Debbie to sign the appropriate papers, in spite of the fact that Debbie lived quite a distance away and had effectively relinquished all parenting responsibilities for Maria to Rhonda and Daniel.

Needless to say, all this created tension in the family. Rhonda realized that she would need to have legal custody of Maria in order to obtain medical care for her, enroll her in school, and make any legally valid decisions for her. Debbie did not want to give up custody of Maria, but she had little recourse because she was not in a position to raise her own daughter. This upset everyone, and it made the situation seem quite "final." At this point, it was impossible to deny that Debbie would not raise her own daughter; moreover, it was obvious that Debbie's parents, Rhonda and Daniel, would be responsible for Maria, for the foreseeable future—that, in effect, they would be Maria's parents, not her grandparents.

Once Debbie signed the papers giving custody of Maria to her parents, Rhonda and Daniel changed Maria's last name to the family's surname. This led to less legal confusion and problems, and it also helped Maria feel like a "real" member of the family.

Rhonda further described how critical the courts were of her and Daniel as they worked to gain custody of Maria. One of the court officials asked them why they felt they could successfully raise Maria when they obviously failed raising Debbie. Rhonda distinctly felt that the underlying question opinion of the legal system was: "You didn't do it right with your own child. What makes you think you can do it right this time?"

As mentioned previously throughout this book, Rhonda is not the only grandparent who faced this issue. Many parenting grandparents interviewed talked about how judged and criticized they felt, not just by the legal system, but by doctors, teachers, other parents and grandparents, including some of their own friends. Several grandparents shared that the mere fact that grandchildren live with their grandparents suggests to observers that something is very "wrong."

Far too many parenting grandparents feel worn down by the legal system, reluctant to ask for help from social-service agencies for fear that these agencies will take their grandchildren away from them. Without legal guardianship or custody, which many adult parents refuse to give, parenting grandparents are often stuck between the proverbial "rock and hard place." Yet they are not willing turn their backs on their grandchildren, giving them to strangers to raise—no matter how hard the fight becomes, grandparents fight for their grandchildren. This singular commitment is manifested universally, over and over again.

To balance the scales here, some grandparents interviewed did share positive experiences. One recurring theme came from the grandfathers, who talked about how much they enjoyed getting involved with their grandchildren's school activities. They felt proud to be involved with their grandchildren in this way, especially because most of them had been absorbed by their work or careers when their own children were growing up, and so they had been unable to attend school events during the day. Being able to go on school trips, participate in classroom activities, and attend school sporting events made these grandfathers— and their grandchildren—very happy. For some of these grandfathers, this was a whole new experience, as it was for many of the formerly neglected grandchildren, as well.

Once again, let's return to Maria's story.

Maria's grandfather, Daniel, learned how to braid her hair, something he had never done for his own daughters. He also made Maria's school lunches, helped her with her homework, and often walked her to and from school—again, all things he had missed out on with his own daughters because he had been at work. These are sacred moments spent with your grandchildren. Despite the formidable challenges parenting grandparents face, the moments experienced in and from the heart—the soft moments emerging from deep connections to your grandchildren—are unique moments to treasure, and the memories they create last a lifetime.

Rhonda's experience was somewhat different from Daniel's. She candidly shared how frightened she was to take on the responsibility of raising Maria. Several times, Rhonda mentioned that her husband became her inspiration. At the age of fifty-five, Daniel lost his job, and he could not find another one. Instead of sinking into the weight of the financial strain—exacerbated by having an additional child to raise—Daniel and Rhonda consciously worked on their attitude, deciding to see their family situation as an opportunity, rather than a burden. However, Rhonda insisted that she was able to manage her own attitude only because her husband so inspired her.

As Maria grew older, Rhonda said her daughters, Carol and Jane (Maria's aunts) became pretty helpful, and one of them even began to take Maria for three to four weeks during the summer in order to give Rhonda and Daniel some respite.

As Rhonda related their story, it became clear that she and Daniel supported each other throughout the process by openly communicating their own needs to each other. They did not shrink from the challenges they faced; instead, they took them on with full awareness, allowing their family values and beliefs to guide their way.

Even when they had to make tough decisions related to their daughter, Debbie (Maria's mother), they shared their fears, disappointments, and frustrations with each other, always guided by what they believed. At times, their decisions reflected "tough love," but, in their hearts, they never stopped caring about and loving Debbie—even when they had to tell Debbie not to call anymore, because it was too upsetting for Maria. For Maria, each call was a reminder that her biological mother was out in the world somewhere choosing not to raise her.

Children and teens do not, and cannot, fill in the details of the issues and demons that their biological and/or adoptive parent(s) might have to wrestle. Not having the internal resources that adults have, all kids and teens in these situations know is that their parent(s) have abandoned and rejected them; they are alive, but do not care enough about the kids to raise them. Sometimes children even will come to a conclusion as to why their parents have left them—and, far too frequently, that conclusion is about their not being lovable, not being good enough, or not being normal. This illustrates why it is so important to seek counseling for your grandchildren in order to make sure that they don't grow up believing these wrong conclusions, which will negatively impact every life decision they make as adults.

Sometimes no amount of caring and loving is enough to help our troubled adult children turn their lives around. Internally, we experience an indescribable sorrow, which we must move beyond in order to raise our grandchildren. But that does not mean our sorrow and sense of loss disappear; it only means that we must move beyond our feelings, because we have no other choice. This may be the most difficult of all the challenges that parenting grandparents face.

Let us return to Maria's story.

When Maria was fourteen years old, Daniel was diagnosed with cancer. Ever since losing his job years before, Daniel had been a stay-at-home dad, and Rhonda worked outside the home. The reversal of their traditional roles added another dimension to parenting Maria, but they were able to make it work.

However, facing the possibility of her grandfather's death was devastating for Maria. Up to this time, Daniel and Rhonda had custody of Maria, but they had not officially adopted her. Without the adoption, Maria would not receive any death benefits. Daniel's health declined rapidly, and he and Rhonda now had the additional challenge of going through the adoption process. Daniel died one day after signing all the necessary official adoption papers. Maria was fifteen years old when the adoption became official, entitling her to Daniel's death benefits.

Understandably, Daniel's death triggered all of Maria's abandonment issues. She had never met or known her biological father, and now, the only father she ever knew had died. Maria described having the constant thought, "My dad died; my biological mother left me; my biological father has never been in my life. What's wrong with me?"

After Daniel's death, Maria admitted that she started acting out. After Maria received a diagnosis of ADHD (Attention Deficit Hyperactivity Disorder; for more information, refer to chapter 7), the school assigned tutors to work with her, but Maria admitted that they just made her angry. In fact, Maria said she was pretty mean to them, especially the female tutors. Even today, she still is not sure why she was so aggressive toward her tutors. "I figure it had something to do with Debbie," was all she said.

On the other hand, Maria considered men evil, intensely disliking all of them except for her grandfather. She said her emotions against men became stronger after Daniel's death. Again, she does not understand why, but, when she looks back, she realizes she just thought they were all "bad."

It's interesting to note that, following Daniel's death, Maria began to have school problems, which led to her ADHD diagnosis. Many times, the painful losses our grandchildren endure may cause them to have both concentration and behavioral problems. But, in fact, they may be experiencing something called complicated mourning. Dr. James A. Fogarty, a licensed clinical psychologist, discusses this in his book, entitled *The Magical Thoughts of Grieving Children: Treating Children with Complicated Mourning and Advice for Parents.* Significantly, Dr. Fogarty discusses how easy it is to confuse complicated mourning with ADHD.

Fogarty terms the behaviors that resemble ADHD *commotion*: "Commotion is a behavior exhibited by bereaved children and adolescents based on the combination of excessive energy, attentional difficulties, tension, and fear that children display when experiencing grief reactions."[24]

Commotion is a good descriptor, because many children demonstrate this reaction through very active behaviors that resemble ADHD. This possible misdiagnosis can lead to your grandchildren receiving unnecessary medications, as well as having to deal with the ramifications of a negative label that will follow them through school.[25]

Therefore, if you notice excessive energy, feelings of frailty, tension, or fear in your grandchildren following the death of or separation from a loved one, seek the help of a mental-health professional. Ask him or her to do a comprehensive history of your grandchildren's development, including all loss experiences, which will help in the determination of the existence of commotion reactions associated with grief. Administering appropriate cognitive and neuropsychological evaluations will also assist in ruling out or confirming the diagnosis of ADHD in your grandchildren.

Back to Maria's story, once again.

Following Daniel's death and the emergence of Maria's troubling behaviors, Rhonda joined a hospice support group to help her cope with her own spousal grief, and she also found a support group for Maria, one that helped children who had experienced significant losses in their lives.

Maria described having shared a lot of her feelings with the other teens in her support group. She emphasized how she was able to talk about her emotions related to her birth mother and father, and she believes being in this group kept her from getting into deeper trouble after Daniel died. Her rebellious behaviors lasted for about a year, after which time she was able to feel safe and secure again.

Maria also told me that one of her biggest fears growing up was that she would be taken away from her grandparents. To manage her fears, she slept with a light on until she was twelve. In addition, she would fall asleep in her grandparent's bed, and then they moved her to her own bed later on in the night. When she bathed or showered, she had to leave the bathroom door wide open, so that she could sing or talk to them the entire time.

Going to school was a big issue for a while because of her fear of being taken away from her grandparents. Every year, Maria insisted that Rhonda and Daniel talk not only to the school principal, but also to all her teachers, so that they would know what to do if her biological mother or father showed up.

All these precautions helped Maria achieve as much of a sense of safety and security as was possible. It is interesting and important to note that, as Maria entered junior high school, she began to orchestrate the actions she expected her grandparents and her school to take in order to keep her safe.

It is important to encourage your grandchildren to become proactive about satisfying their needs for safety and security. This will empower them and reduce a lot of the tension that they experience from their real or imagined fear of being taken away from you. It will also reduce some of the need to be rebellious—whether they exhibit "acting out" or "acting in" behaviors. Adolescence is a time of tremendous physical and emotional changes. When loss, abandonment, neglect, or trauma occurs during this period, as Maria put it, "A whole bunch of bad stuff can happen."

Maria explained that, at the height of her rebellion, she wanted to be like Daniel, whom she perceived as "not having any feelings." She just did not want to feel anything. Yet, as time passed following his death, one of Maria's insights was the realization that Daniel did have emotions, and she added, "Hey, pretending you don't have any feelings just does not work." It's hard to really shut down our feelings, and, when we do, the price is a disconnection from our inner self, our heart. The cost is too high, even for adults, but, for children or adolescents, it often seems to be the best way to handle the searing pain of abandonment.

One other major issue that Maria grappled with following Daniel's death was receiving telephone calls from her biological mother, Debbie. Maria said, "Every call was a trigger that just set off a whole range of bad feelings." Whenever Debbie called, Maria did not want to talk to her, and she did not accept the birthday gifts that Debbie sent her, either. Despite the demonstrated hostility born of the pain of abandonment, Maria admits to "bawling like a baby," when she overheard Rhonda telling someone that Debbie was in jail.

When asked what it was about Debbie's calls that brought up so much fury within her, Maria replied, "They were too much of a reminder of being deserted. I mean, almost as soon as I was born, she just took off. I never met my biological father; I don't even know anything about him. My biological parents are alive—they are out there somewhere, but they didn't care enough about me to raise me, and they don't care enough about me to be in my life now."

Clearly, talking about her biological mother was still very painful for Maria. At the time of her interview, she was eighteen years old, yet the pain of her abandonment was still very raw. Maria's words all had one main theme: Debbie was never there for her, never helped her through anything. Maria could not even acknowledge Debbie as the woman who gave birth to her. At one point in the interview, she said, "The only good thing Debbie did was to give birth to me, and, even that, I think my real mom, Rhonda, did. Again, I am going to pretend."

We see here an example of the magical thinking that Dr. Fogarty describes, again. in his book, *The Magical Thoughts of Grieving Children.* Fogarty defines *magical thought* as "children's inaccurate conclusion(s) regarding a loss experience, resulting in children believing that they are responsible for the loss experience and need to fix the loss experience."[26]

By making Rhonda her birth mother and not just her adoptive mother, Maria internally feels wanted and loved, and she has a sense of belonging. This deflects the pain of her birth to parents who, in her mind, did not want her. This softens the raw, deep pain of not only abandonment, but also having to face the question: "What was so wrong with me they did not want me?"

Maria continued, "A birthday is supposed to be a happy day. Think happy birthday, not crappy birthday. I was, and still am, so angry with her." Before her adoption, Maria pretended to be nice to Debbie when she called. Maria described that, "Sometimes, I even told her stuff to make her happy." This might seem confusing, but Maria explained it simply: "I was so afraid she would come and take me away or send someone to get me, so I just pretended." But once Maria's adoption was official, when she was fifteen, she no longer obsessed over this fear. After that, Maria said, "I am done. I can't deal with her anymore. I refused to talk to Debbie. In fact, the last time she called, I told her off. We have not spoken since then."

Maria's adoption was incredibly significant to her. Even though Daniel died before the adoption became official, Maria now felt "legitimate"; she officially had a mother and father, and officially belonged to a family who loved her and wanted her. The adoption closed the door on Maria's insecurities regarding safety and belonging. It eliminated her need to pretend with Debbie, so that Debbie would not take Maria away; it also minimized Maria's magical thinking, but it did not eliminate it entirely.

Perhaps most important of all, it helped Maria realize that the trouble she was experiencing as a teen—skipping school, failing grades, smoking, withdrawing and isolating herself, hanging out with peers who were a negative influence, and so on—was an all-too-similar road to the one Debbie had been on as a teen. Because of the strength of her relationship with Rhonda and Daniel (even though he had since died), and their ability to meet her needs for love and belonging, Maria made a conscious decision to be different from her birth mother. In fact, Maria said, "I just am not going to be that way."

Again, through the story of Rhonda, Daniel, and Maria, we see the powerful bond of love and caring between parenting grandparents and their grandchildren, as well as how very influential this bond is. In short, nothing is easy when it comes to raising your grandchildren, yet nothing is more sacred or more noble than raising your grandchildren.

Nevertheless, this story would be incomplete if we did not attend to Daniel and Maria's adult daughter, Debbie, who is now forty-one years old. Unlike so many of the grandparents' troubled adult children who refused to discuss their situations, Debbie recently agreed to an interview. In her own words: "If sharing my story will help just one person out there who is struggling like I did—and like I still am—it will be worth it."

We know very little about the adult children who have lost their way, whom society frequently views as irresponsible, and who appear to lack accountability for their decisions and actions. We see these adult children as negligent parents. We label their behaviors as deviant, sometimes even criminal, behaviors; we judge their addictions and other problems, as well as their promiscuity. These labels and judgments may be accurate, but that does not mean that we know their stories— certainly, we have not walked in their shoes. Quite simply, we usually do not see the person inside. Who are they? What do they think, feel, and believe?

Many of the unstable adult children of parenting grandparents came from what we might term "good" homes, with a solid family structure and a framework of strong morals and values. Many of these adult children have siblings who are successful adults, who did not have the same intense difficulties growing up. Yet they lived in the same home, with the same parents who taught the same values to all their children. We can only wonder why the lives of those struggling adult children turned out so differently from the lives of their siblings.

As mentioned above, Debbie wondered about this, too—so much so that she chose to share her own experiences candidly, hoping to help others. Let us take a glimpse at Debbie's complicated internal world, just as she expressed it in her interview.

> *"I am the middle of three sisters. I was adopted, as was my oldest sister, when I was quite young. Even as a little girl, I felt different. I never felt as good as my older sister who was really smart, or my younger sister who was the 'real' child, always comfortable just being herself. I saw myself as really different, incredibly sensitive, and just always feeling like 'there was something wrong with me'—like I just was 'not good enough.' I was told that I was hyperactive, and I saw a psychiatrist during my preschool years. Later, it seemed to me like I was always going to a doctor, and it made me feel like whatever was wrong with me would never go away.*

"Emotionally, I was always angry, and I always struggled with poor grades in school. I could not handle even the slightest criticism, and, as I got older, I always made a big deal of everything—in my own mind, everything was a crisis. I had a very negative self-image: I thought I was too short and too fat, clothes were hard to buy for me, school was hard for me. I just did not feel there was anything good about me. I started drinking and hanging out with the wrong crowd. I kept seeing myself as fat and never good enough, and so I kept drinking; over time, I became bulimic to prevent more weight gain.

"But, looking back, I realize that I just had this 'twisted thinking' and extreme sensitivity. I couldn't move beyond them. Along with the drinking and bulimia, I had problems at home. I started running away from home because everything was a 'big deal' in our family. But I could not even run away successfully! I would leave in a fit of anger, and then I would return for a while. This pattern just kept repeating itself; the more it did, the more I saw myself as a 'loser.'

"Thinking back to some time before all that, I did have a close relationship with my grandfather. When he was in the hospital dying, I wanted to see him so badly, But, I was too young at only eleven. I kept begging my parents to get me in to see him somehow. It was just the hospital rules back then, but it felt personal to me. To this day, I remember how angry I was that I could not see him. We were so close. When he died, I was devastated. The one person I felt loved and understood me was gone, and I remember feeling really alone. My parents tried everything, from therapy to 'tough love.' Things were really difficult for me after Grandpa died. Not long after that, I started my pattern of running away. I would leave home and come back—and I just kept doing that over and over again. Eventually, my parents said that I had to go to boarding school.

"In order for the state to pay for my school and healthcare, my parents had to testify before the court that they did not want me. Even though they told me ahead of time that they would have to say that in court in order to get financial coverage for my schooling and

health insurance, when they said it out loud in court, I believed it. I felt devastated—again. In essence, my parents gave custody of me to the state because it was the only way available to them at the time to get me the help I needed. I now know that my parents loved me, but, at the time, I was really messed up inside. Hearing my parents say that they didn't want me—knowing that they "gave me up" to the state made me think, 'I am not lovable.' Being adopted, I felt like I was being 'given away' twice—first by my biological parents, and then by my adoptive parents. I felt totally alone, unwanted, unloved, and worthless.

"At seventeen, I became pregnant with Maria. When I was eight months pregnant, I went to live at a home for unwed pregnant women. After Maria was born, I lived at a Florence Crittendon Home, which was a residential treatment facility that provided medical, nutritional, educational, and counseling to women like me, who faced pregnancy and single-mom parenting. I left the home when Maria was six weeks old, and returned to live with my parents. I was now eighteen years old.

"The plan was that my mom could watch Maria while I was at work. I had to work two job to help pay my bills, because, as a high-school dropout I couldn't find any one job that paid enough. At this point, my mother did most of the caretaking for Maria. Again, my 'twisted thinking' kicked in, and I felt my mom was trying to take Maria from me because I was not being a very good mom. No matter what I did, I always had these 'not good enough' feelings.

"Yet, from the day Maria was born, more than anything, I wanted to be a good mom. I tried. I even prayed to be a good mom, but nothing I did worked. I was becoming exhausted from working two jobs and trying to take care of Maria, and I began to feel very depressed. I started to feel so bad inside that it felt like I had no energy to get through the day. That is when I started to use cocaine. It helped me feel less depressed, and it gave me more energy to work both of my jobs. But my drug habit cost so much that I started using

all the money I earned to keep buying cocaine. Before long, I got caught up in this downward spiral, and I couldn't get out of it.

"Looking back, I see that my 'twisted thinking' continued to plague me into my early twenties. When asked to further explain this term, "twisted thinking," which she used frequently to describe herself, Debbie said that it was basically a problem-solving inability on her part.

"For example, I would try to think of ways to earn more money so I would be able to live on my own with my daughter, but then I would just keep doing the same things I'd always done, and I'd still expect it would give me the outcome I wanted."

Debbie even used a quote attributed to Albert Einstein: "Insanity is doing the same things over and over again but expecting different results."

Ruth C. Engs, RN, EdD, Professor of Applied Health Science at Indiana University, offers one of the best descriptions of the addictive process: "Any activity, substance, object, or behavior that has become the major focus of a person's life to the exclusion of other activities, or that has begun to harm the individual or others physically, mentally, or socially, is considered an addictive behavior. A person can become addicted, dependent, or compulsively obsessed with anything."[27]

Furthermore, physical addictions to various chemicals, as well as psychological dependence on certain activities, may produce beta-endorphins in the brain, which makes the person feel "high." Some experts suggest that, if a person continues to engage in the activity in order to achieve this feeling of well-being and euphoria, he or she may enter into an addictive cycle. In so doing, he or she becomes physically addicted to their own brain chemicals. This leads to continuation of the behavior, even though it may have negative physical, emotional, and/or social consequences. However, other experts feel that these are just bad habits.[28]

Let's look at some of Debbie's self-described behaviors and thinking:

- Debbie was obsessed with thinking about how she could get out of her situations: doing poorly at school, running away from home, attempting to get her child back, etc. However, by her own admission, she was addicted to the same behaviors and activities that kept her going in vicious circles, hoping for a different outcome but actually getting the same, undesired results, which she experienced as failure. The tension she felt with failing would start the obsessive thinking process again, and the addictive behaviors would begin, despite her best efforts to break this negative cycle.

- Debbie engaged in aberrant/deviant behaviors, even though this caused harm to herself, her health, her school performance, and her family.

- Debbie compulsively engaged in these activities (promiscuity, using drugs and/or alcohol, skipping school, etc.), repeating them over and over again, even when she did not want to, and she found it difficult to stop.

- Debbie apparently could not control when she would engage in the deviant behaviors and activities, or to what extent or duration she would continue to engage in them once the cycle began.

- Every time Debbie tried to self-correct, despite her best efforts, she would experience withdrawal symptoms— which, for her, included irritability, restlessness, and depression. The withdrawal symptoms caused such extreme discomfort, that she would begin the addictive cycle again in order to ease it. The anxiety and low self-esteem that she experienced were a result of the overwhelming realization she had no control over herself or her environment.

Let's continue Debbie's story, once again, in her own words.

"More than anything, I wanted to be a good mom. When I lost custody of Maria, I felt really lost. I kept thinking, 'How dare my parents take my child?' I was so angry, and, because I couldn't handle my anger, I would drink. And then, while drunk, I would devise in my head this 'big plan' to take Maria: I would get my GED and attend Job Corps, and I would be able to get my daughter back. I met my first husband at Job Corps, and I kept thinking, 'We'll get married, and there will be enough money to raise Maria. I'll stop drinking, and I'll stop using cocaine. I will be a good mom.'

"But then, I got kicked out of Job Corps. Shortly after that, I lost my job. I got so depressed and anxious that I just drank more and more. I started gaining a lot of weight because of the alcohol. At around that same time, my husband went into the military, and I started with the bulimia again like when I was in high school.

"At times, I thought my plans were brilliant; my only thought through all of it was to get my child back. I always held that hope no matter what. Even when I had to sign custody of Maria over to my parents, I could not give up my hope. I thought that, if I signed those papers, they would let me see her. I always had that 'twisted thinking'; I convinced myself that I could make things work out, somehow—even though I kept repeating the same mistakes, and couldn't stop. I didn't know how to stop.

"When I could no longer see Maria, my life just completely fell apart. I lost all hope; I had nothing to live for. I was unemployed, my husband was in the military, and I became seriously depressed. I was totally alone and lonely. At that point, I did whatever I had to do in order to get drugs and buy alcohol. I never thought my life could get any worse than it had been up to that point—but it did.

"I began stealing to support my habits. I was caught during a robbery and wound up in jail. To make it even worse, it was three days before Maria's birthday—and I was in jail. When I got out, I knew I had to leave the town where I'd grown up. The only thing that ever comforted me was the water, so I moved to be near the ocean.

"But all I did was take my problems with me—along with my depression, my 'twisted thinking,' my self-loathing, and all my addictions. Twenty years passed, during which time, I would call my parents and my daughter. My calls only created turmoil for them, and my mom asked me to stop calling, for Maria's sake.

"I was tired of trying so hard to get my life together, and continually failing. I was tired of being alone, tired of standing on street corners and living in abandoned houses, tired of trying to figure out where and how I would get my next fix. I was tired of all of it. But, more than anything, I was tired of feeling guilty about my daughter, and it deeply saddened me that I had not seen her in over twenty years.

"I had been talking about getting my life together with a lady from a storefront church down the street from where I prostituted. She said to me, 'Debbie, what are you doing? There is nothing it seems I can do for you but pray for you, and I will do that.' Shortly after that, I was arrested again—this time for prostitution. Basically, they just made me pay a fine and do community service, plus enter a court-mandated substance-abuse recovery program. At the program, I met a man named Sonny, who was trying to put his own life back together. We became friends and tried to help each other get better. We were able to help each other "use less," but neither one of us could break our addictions, even with the help the program offered.

"Sonny and I started living together—we squatted in abandoned houses—and I remember this one morning, a few years ago, when I was waking up and saw that Sonny had gone out. I stood up and looked around. I just stood there and thought to myself, 'I have no power, no family, no daughter, no decent friends, no work. I have *nothing.' I still can remember standing in the middle of that cold, dilapidated house, and just crying out to God to help me, because I realized I had nothing to live for. Absolutely nothing.*

"And then I remembered the lady from the storefront church, the one who said she would pray for me. I went to the church and found out they had a program for addicts. I started going to meetings and studying the Bible. I joined a special program for women. Slowly, I began to let go of my old friends, who were such a negative influence in my life, and I began to make new friends, people who cared about my health and well-being. It was hard, and I faced a lot of trials.

"I found a job but soon discovered my new workplace was full of 'potheads.' When I started this job, I had been clean for only three weeks, but I realized that the longer I stayed clean, the more into the recovery philosophy I found myself. Sonny and I were still together, and he was doing better, too. The more we saw ourselves and each other doing better, the more it encouraged us to keep at it. We really started supporting each other's progress, and we realized that we could only be helped by a power far greater than ourselves.

"Right now, I feel terrible about the choices I have made in the past. I feel stupid when I see that I refused to let go of my 'twisted thinking'—if only I could have seen sooner that I needed to trust God and not myself! When I look back, I see that any constructive feedback anyone gave me triggered my 'twisted thinking.' I would immediately react to whatever they said with, 'Something is wrong with me!'

"A couple of years ago, I was a tramp. I had no idea how my decisions and actions affected others. I feel like I have more now than I could have asked God for. More than anything in the world, I regret the pain I have caused my family, especially my daughter, Maria."

Shortly after the interview Debbie wrote me this note:

"I wanted to thank you for allowing me the opportunity to give something back. I want you to understand that I am very grateful to my parents for raising Maria and my sisters. While I was out trying and not coming through, they did come through. And Maria has turned out beautifully. Thank God for them."

No doubt, parenting grandparents, you can relate to this family's story, which conveys all the loss, turmoil, broken hearts, and emotional pain so frequently experienced in these circumstances, as well as all the courage, hope, and healing that overcoming these experiences demands. This story's position at the end of the book was deliberate: Its purpose was to let each and every parenting grandparent reading this book know that, besides the love and care you continually give your grandchildren, you also set an example that empowers them to hold onto the hope of leading a fulfilling life—and you inspire them to go beyond that, to not merely hope to lead that life, but to make it happen. In addition, despite the tough love and painful decisions that you had to make regarding your troubled adult children, you also have shown your grandchildren that love and caring is the most important ingredient when raising children, and this is what they will model when they raise their own children.

Not all of your stories may have happy endings, but many of them will—and this is the very reason that requires you to stay confident, courageous, and hopeful. Despite all the obstacles, challenges, problems, turmoil, angst, frustration, fear, and anxiety that Rhonda, Daniel, and their family had to endure, they remained hopeful. Even Debbie, during her lowest moments, remained hopeful. It takes courage to stay hopeful in the face of overwhelming odds, to be sure; however, by this point in time, you already have experienced a lifetime of courageous moments, and these will serve you well as you raise your grandchildren—and also grieve for your own adult children.

Let's finish this chapter with an update on Rhonda and Daniel's family.

Rhonda began dating Albert, a man she met in the hospice support group she joined after Daniel's death. After two years of dating, Rhonda and Albert married. Currently, they are enjoying their own children and grandchildren, and the stepchildren and step-grandchildren they now have as a result of their marriage.

Maria is now twenty-four years old and engaged to be married. After high school, Maria went to college, but, after finishing her first semester, she decided that college was not for her. Instead, her deep love for animals led to her starting her own pet-sitting business, which is currently very successful. Maria also works as a nanny from time to time, and she teaches ice-skating in the evenings.

Debbie is now married to Sonny, and they both are employed and have been "clean and sober" from drugs for two years. They both also continue to participate in their support groups. Debbie is studying to become a medical assistant, but she continues to work full-time.

★ ★ ★ ★ ★ ★

As Debbie began to heal, she started calling Rhonda more often. Rhonda received Debbie's calls and began to notice a big shift in her daughter. According to her, Debbie was becoming more sensitive to what was happening to various family members, more compassionate, and softer in her emotions. Debbie became more outward-directed. She would inquire about family members, including Maria.

After one year of weekly phone conversations, Rhonda and Debbie decided to see each other. Debbie had been drug-free for a year at that point, and both women had a deep need and desire to reunite. It had been more than twenty years since mother and daughter had been in each other's presence, and they both were excited, nervous, anxious, and scared. They decided to meet in a neutral place halfway between each of their homes.

Rhonda and Albert arrived at the designated meeting place at the appointed time. As time passed, Rhonda worried that Debbie and Sonny would not show up. She admitted to feeling scared about what would happen when they did show up, and also what would happen if they did not show up. Suddenly, in the rearview mirror, Rhonda saw a car pull up and park. She knew it was Debbie and Sonny.

As Rhonda and Albert exited their car, Rhonda could hear Debbie screaming, "My mother, my mother," as she ran toward her. The two women could not stop embracing each other. In an instant, the years of anguish, rejection, addictive behaviors, disagreements, legal battles—and all the forms of pain that had resulted from the situation—all dissolved in their mutually loving and healing embrace.

Rhonda said that she couldn't remember the last time she had seen Debbie looking so healthy. Debbie's hair glistened in the sun, and Rhonda could not stop touching it. Sonny and Albert stood off to the side, watching mother and daughter come together in a way they had not believed could ever happen.

Sonny brought roses for Rhonda, and Albert greeted Debbie with an open heart. They shared a meal together, looked at some family pictures, and said a prayer of reunification. In two hours' time, they had begun the journey of healing their family, now torn apart for more than twenty years. Rhonda and Debbie talk every day now, and they are planning another, longer visit with each other.

According to Rhonda, Debbie's transformation has affected everyone in the family differently. Debbie has re-established contact with her younger sister, Jane, but not with her older sister, Carol. Debbie and Maria have not reconnected as of this writing. Maria is not even willing to talk to Rhonda about Debbie—let alone talk to Debbie herself. In fact, Maria wants nothing to do with Debbie at all.

Realizing that she missed Maria's entire life, Debbie experiences deep sorrow: "I feel terrible about choices I have made in the past." Tearfully, Debbie repeated what she had shared earlier. "Two years ago, I was a tramp. I never thought about how my actions affected others. I can't even find the words to describe how stupid I was for not letting go of my 'twisted thinking.' If only I had trusted God and not myself."

Debbie feels deep and sincere remorse for not being a mother to Maria, for being the cause of so much of her daughter's pain—and her parent's pain—for so many years. She shared that she will spend a very long time trying to forgive herself, while also praying for Maria's forgiveness.

Despite these difficult insights, Debbie is able to realize that, today, she has more than she could have asked God for: "My mother is back in my life, and my younger sister, Jane, e-mails me. I have a great stepfather, a wonderful husband, a fat cat, and a big yard." With deep gratitude, Debbie credits the woman from the storefront church with the healing shift that her own life has taken: "She never judged me, she just kept telling me, every time she saw me, that she would pray for me. She touched my heart so deeply, because she accepted me just as I was."

Rhonda has been clear about her feelings with Maria. Debbie is her daughter, Rhonda has explained, and, despite the many difficult years of anguish, Rhonda has told Maria, "I have a need for Debbie, and that will never change."

This could have been a very complicated and difficult position for Rhonda to be in, but her clarity about the place both Maria and Debbie have in her life has kept the situation from becoming enmeshed. Although it remains difficult for Maria, she has accepted Rhonda's feelings. Maria values her relationship with Rhonda, and the two of them remain close and loving.

This family's story, like every story in this book, tells of hope, courage, and healing. What distinguishes this particular story is that it came "full circle," with the re-entry of Debbie into the family. Unfortunately, not all grandparents experience the healing of their adult child. Sadly, some adult children have died, some remain in prison, some have addictions or mental-health challenges that they have not overcome, and some have just given up.

What Debbie has helped us see and understand is that most of the demons she battled were internal. This is true of most struggling adult children. What is equally true for most of them, like Debbie, is that, although the external world may have exacerbated certain of the struggles and personal challenges, the empathy of others—or even of one other person—often makes all the difference.

For Debbie, it was the woman from the storefront church, who prayed for Debbie instead of judging her. The person who "makes all the difference" exists for everyone who struggles to overcome inner demons of any kind. It is our ability as individuals to truly recognize and empathize with our fellow human beings, regardless of their challenges that is such an important aspect of everyone's healing.

The word *healing* means to "make whole." To truly heal ourselves, we first must become self-aware. We cannot blame others, we cannot cast ourselves as "victims" when we greet the world, and we cannot pretend everything is okay when it is not. Self-awareness takes a great deal of courage.

When we are self-aware, we don't try to fool ourselves or other people. We accept who we are and what we have done. We are accountable for all our decisions—whether successes or failures. It is only from this place of self-awareness, which, in turn, leads to true self-acceptance, that we can live in the integrity of our own truth.

It is in this place of integrity that we can plant, and then cultivate, the seed of forgiveness. The story that Debbie and Rhonda shared offer us a lesson of both self-forgiveness *and* forgiveness. So many years of pain and anguish—upheaval, addiction, fear, worry, rejection, and even abandonment—at long last, have given way to healing and hope for each of these women. Maria is at a different point in the journey: for her, a reconciliation with Debbie may take a long time; in fact, it may never happen.

Each of us heals in our own time and in our own way. What is important is that each of them found a path to personal integrity, and each of them has experienced personal transformation, in a way that reflects her own needs, strengths, vulnerabilities, courage, and beliefs.

CONCLUSION

It has been both an honor and a gratifying experience to research and write this book. In doing so, so many lives have touched mine, across the boundaries of geography, cultures, and generations. I have learned so much about living from the heart. The underpinning to each and every story in this book has been the deep and abiding love of grandparents for their grandchildren—and the sacrifices that all those grandparents so willingly make in order to raise their grandchildren.

To end this book, allow me to talk about raising the "spirit" of your grandchildren. We have talked about raising your grandchildren in every other way—physically, mentally, emotionally, and socially. We have discussed support systems and resources to make your parenting role easier. We have reviewed the developmental life stages, as well as the tasks associated with each stage that you and your grandchildren must master in order to proceed to the next stage of life. We have read the stories of parenting grandparents, which you have so generously allowed me to share from your interviews. All this aided me immeasurably in making the material of this book more meaningful and relevant, and I am grateful.

Now I wish to offer some brief thoughts about spirit. We each have a unique spirit that is our life force—the energy of our being, which is our essence. This connects us with all of life; thus, in spirit, we are never alone. However, our spirit needs sustenance, nurturing, and love.

Your selfless decision to raise your grandchildren was a decision first born in your spirit; your life-force energy realizing that the life-force energy of your grandchildren might be diminished if not for you. Because of this, by loving and caring for your grandchildren, you uplift their spirits. Spirit is the one resource we need to "thrive" in life. We can "get by" with just mental and physical energy; however, in order to thrive and flourish, our spirit must propel us. This is yet another reason why raising your grandchildren is such sacred and noble work.

As I complete this book, I think of the words of Elisabeth Kübler-Ross, who wrote so brilliantly about grief and loss: "If you shield the mountain from the windstorm, you will never see the beauty of the carvings made by the windstorm." Many of you, as parenting grandparents, have experienced life's windstorms as you raised, and continue to raise, your grandchildren. Let me gently remind you to reflect on the beauty of the souls of your grandchildren of all ages, as well as on your own souls, as you love, nurture, and raise them.

Let me also gently remind you of the importance of your grandchildren's daily experience of your unconditional love for and devotion to them. Finally, allow me to share these wise words from the business card of a colleague who has allowed me to share them with you. In a simple way, these words capture the sacredness of each day you spend raising your grandchildren:

> *This bright new day, complete with 24 hours of opportunities, choices, and attitudes is a perfectly matched set of 1,440 minutes. This unique gift, this one day, cannot be exchanged, replaced, or refunded. Handle with care. Make the most of it. There is only one to a person!"*

Is what you are doing making a difference in your grandchildren's lives? Yes. Is what you are doing making a difference in the world? Yes. Is what you are doing sacred and noble? Yes. Is what you are doing making the most of each day—all twenty-four hours of it? Yes.

With humility, I express my gratitude to all you parenting grandparents, who, somewhere in the world, are making a bright, new day for all your grandchildren—and our grandchildren are the future generation of our world.

"Love is the core energy that rules everything....love is the one ingredient that holds us all together." John E. Fetzer

ABOUT THE AUTHOR

Elaine K. Williams, LMSW, CHt, is a nationally respected coach, counselor and workshop/retreat facilitator. She is known for her common sense approach to developing and expanding human potential. Her focus is on personal and spiritual self-development for children and adults.

Elaine's work is guided by inspiration and inner-knowing. Both are urgings from the deep self that tell us what it will take to make our life meaningful. Any leap that we want to make in our personal or professional life that aligns with our passion and sense of purpose, and with our deepest values, is by definition meaningful.

This belief forms the basis of Elaine's work as a coach and counselor, national speaker, author/writer, and national trainer/facilitator. For more information about Elaine and her work, visit www.Elainekwilliams. com; to receive her monthly newsletter, write her at Elainekwilliams@ aol.com.

NOTES

1. Seniorjournal.com, http://www.census.gov/population/ www/socdemo/hh-fam/cps2009.html, Table C4, September 12, 2010.

2. www.foxnews.com/us/2010/09/09*Sharp Rise Reported in Number of Grandparents Raising Their Grandchildren,* Pew Center: http://pewsocialtrends.org/

3. Ibid.

4. AARP Foundation, *State Fact Sheets for Grandparents and Other Relatives Raising Children,* www.grandfactsheets.org/ state_fact_sheets.cfm (October 2007).

5. The Silent Generation, http://www.en.wikipedia.org/wiki/ Silent_Generation, (last modified 11 February 2011).

6. The Baby Boomer Generation, http://www.en.wikipedia. org/wiki/Baby_boomer (last modified 23 February 2011.

7. Generation X, http://www.en.wikipedia.org/wiki/ Generation_X (last modified 3 February 2011).

8. Generation Y, http://www.en.wikipedia.org/wiki/ Generation_Y (last modified 5 March 2011).

9. Children of Prisoners Library, http://www.fcnetwork.org./cpl/cplindex.html.

10. Ibid.

11. The National Resource Center on Children and Families of the Incarcerated at Family and Corrections Network, http://www.fcnetwork.org/, Fact Sheets, NRCCFI at FCN 2009.

12. "Resilience of Girls with Incarcerated Mothers: The Impact of Girl Scouts," *The Prevention Researcher,* vol. 3, no. 2 (April 2006): 11–14. (http://www.tpronline.org/articles.cfm?articleID=424;

http://www.members.mcpsupport.com/Documents/MCP-Introduction.pdf).

13. "Erikson's Psychosocial Stages Summary Chart," *Erikson's Stages of Psychosocial Development,* psychology.about.com/library/bl_psychosocial_summary.htm-.

14. Blakemore and Choudhury, "Development of the Adolescent Brain: Implications for Executive Function and Social Cognition," *Journal of Child Psychology and Psychiatry* 47:3/4 (2006): 296–312.

15. Daniel Goleman, *Social Intelligence: The Revolutionary New Science of Human Relationships,* (New York: Bantam Books, 2007), 162–86.

16. Post-Traumatic Stress Disorder (PTSD), www.nimh.nih.gov/health/topics/post-traumatic-stress-.

17. "Maslow's Hierarchy of Needs," psychology.about.com, *Psychology Dictionary,* H Index –.

18. William Bridges, *Transitions: Making Sense of Life's Changes*, (Reading, Mass.: Addison-Wesley Publishing Company, 1980).

19. Linda J. Schupp, PhD, *Assessing and Treating Trauma and PTSD,* (Eau Claire, Wis.: PESI, LLC, 2004), 13.

20. Ibid.

21. Karyn Purvis, PhD, and David Cross, PhD, "Caught Between the Amygdala and a Hard Place," *Fostering Families Today* (Nov/Dec 2006): 6.

22. Ibid., 4.

23. Ibid., 6.

24. James A. Fogarty, EdD, *The Magical Thoughts of Grieving Children*, (Amityville, New York: Baywood Publishing Company, Inc., 2000), 9.

25. Ibid., 12.

26. Ibid., 1.

27. Adapted from Ruth C. Engs, RN,EdD, *Alcohol and Other Drugs: Self Responsibility, What Are Addictive Behaviors,* (Bloomington, Ind.: Tichenor Publishing Company, 1996).

28. Ibid.